THE RESTORATION PROJECT

FORFEIT

CLIVE STEPHENS

CRANTHORPE
MILLNER
PUBLISHERS

Copyright © Clive Stephens (2026)

The right of Clive Stephens to be identified as author of this work has been asserted by them in accordance with section 77 and 78 of the Copyright, Designs and Patents Act 1988.

All rights reserved. No part of this publication may be reproduced, stored in a retrieval system, or transmitted in any form or by any means, electronic, mechanical, photocopying, recording, or otherwise, without the prior permission of the publishers.

Any person who commits any unauthorised act in relation to this publication may be liable to criminal prosecution and civil claims for damages.

This book is a work of fiction. Names, characters, places and incidents are either products of the author's imagination or are used fictitiously. Any resemblance to actual events or locales or persons, living or dead, is entirely coincidental.

First published by Cranthorpe Millner Publishers (2026)

ISBN 978-1-80378-342-0 (Paperback)

www.cranthorpemillner.com

Cranthorpe Millner Publishers

FORFEIT

Losing a game of chess by breaking rules, by absence, or by exceeding the time control.

CHAPTER 1

Sally woke up in her own room, facing the wall where, on the other side, she imagined Jason was sleeping. She tried to figure out what homework she did last night. When it didn't immediately arrive in her mind, it bothered her enough to sit up and check her desk, which looked neat and organised, as always.

"Cleanliness is next to godliness," she could imagine her mother saying. Most often in front of guests.

With the organisation pressed upon her by her church-going father, Sally wondered if the angels spoke in alphabetical order. Her parents had barred her from going round to some people's houses, especially to Jason's. They said it was to keep her safe. From what, they didn't say. When Sally asked Jason to describe his room, it sounded the same as hers but after the bomb had hit. She reckoned he didn't have *in* and *out* trays.

She felt the coolness in the air. Her parents told her that warmth meant comfort and that was a fast track to laziness. She could never work out why it was always warmer when they had visitors.

Won't they think we are lazy?

She kept such thoughts to herself. Her parents wouldn't thank her for them.

There was a glass of water on the desk. The yellow and blue butterflies were her favourite pattern. She saw it rarely. Something must have gone well yesterday for her even to see it, let alone have it in her room. This was a good sign. She picked it up and looked through the butterflies. She liked to line up the colours. The yellow on one side and blue on the other meant she would see green. Each move she made to the glass resulted in this. She awarded herself a smile. Having the glass was good, but it was the pinnacle of the mountain from which all paths led down.

The opening bars of 'Eine Kleine Nachtmusik' fired up to tell her someone was calling. The name on the screen was Suzanne. She jerked out a hand to reach for her phone and grabbed its slender metallic edge, only to fumble it. The second time she put thumb and fingers on the edge, it slipped away from her. Only on a focused third attempt, did she successfully pick it up. Except, by then, the call had ended. As she held the phone in her hand, she contemplated ringing back. Any other caller, especially the girls her parents approved of, would have rung her back within a minute to talk about homework. How dull. She hoped they'd invite her to come over, to work on it together.

Her parents thought her phone would be a good way to keep in touch, although only with like-minded daughters. There was no room in her phone for sons. As her parents didn't want her to stare at it all night, she had to hand it over before bed. She quickly learned what that was all about, when Jason's number wasn't there, one morning. Of course, Sally had said nothing at the breakfast table. Instead, when she asked him for it again later that day, he wasn't to know that, this time, she went in the contacts under 'Jane'. The proof in the pudding was the morning after, when the name and number were still there. Simon's alter ego was Suzanne. Simone would have been too obvious and she knew of no one else called Suzanne, so it stood out from the crowd. Much like Simon.

Sally put the phone down for the moment and went back to her homework. He didn't ring back immediately because he didn't know who had the phone. He would try again later. She sipped the water and put the glass down on a wooden coaster. She settled on the chair and began flicking through the pages of notes. It all seemed familiar, but it was the algebra that was foremost in her mind. She picked up a pencil and rewrote the formula. Sometime later, the understanding slipped away from her. She looked back to the top of the page where, at one point, it had all made sense but now looked to have been written backwards. She leaned back a moment, lifted her head up to look at the ceiling and grabbed another quick drink.

The page blurred back into focus and she carried on, after a review of the situation. Soon enough, it slipped away from her again. Again, she leaned back, stretched her head upwards and picked up the glass.

It isn't coming back, so what am I missing?

Now, not even the symbols made sense and there was a feeling of dread lurking in the background. What if her father came in and asked to see her homework? Would she be able to explain it?

She looked at the glass. The butterflies wouldn't line up this time, no matter how she turned it. Her mouth started to feel dry. She only needed a sip. Just a little one and it would be all right. She noticed her fingers were curled up into fists. Relaxing her hands was just as hard as stretching them out.

What was in this water? Was it powered by butterflies? Another thought, a more treacherous one, assailed her. *What had mum put in this drink?*

There was an answer, but to reach it resulted in her reeling in dizziness as she stood up.

This is insane.

She changed tack and made it to the windows but both were locked. That made even less sense. Her parents were keen on her breathing fresh air, despite rarely letting her outside to experience it. She tried to relax but, when she opened her eyes, the glass was halfway to her lips. The dryness escalated to an almost unquenchable thirst. The situation was out of control.

In the end, she gave in and raised it up. As she pressed the rim to her lips and angled up the bottom, she felt her body relax. She couldn't let go. Within a second, all the water was out but, at the last second, her head turned aside and escaped the danger zone. The contents of the glass fell to the carpet. Her feet danced out of the way, too, in case any splashed her. The stress eased. It felt good to be able to put down the glass. It hit the desk heavily and fell over, loudly on its side. She backed away from the table. Only when she felt the bed against the back of her legs did she stop and sit down. As she looked down at herself, she noticed she wasn't wearing pyjamas.

That's odd. How did I manage to go to bed without changing? Well, if I'm dressed, then I should be able to go out.

She stood up and moved towards the door but the handle wouldn't turn. At that point, she offered up some of her thoughts on the sacrificial altar of sound, daring to be heard and judged for her interpretation of the situation.

"I'm curious to know what can make water so addictive that I cannot even put it down, after a few sips."

There was a silence broken only by her phone buzzing with a text. She glanced in its direction but didn't move towards it.

"Is there something in my drink?"

The light faded a moment but returned to its usual brightness soon after.

"If you're thinking of leaving me in the dark, you're too late."

The door opened inwards impolitely and a short but strong-looking woman strode in, wearing business dress under a white lab coat. Sally began to demand what was going on but the lady wasn't interested. She grabbed Sally's arm and dragged her out.

The last sight Sally had of the space that looked like her

bedroom was of the walls closing in. She found herself in a short corridor. Here, cleanliness was the goal. God may have been in this corridor, but not in spirit. It was clean without being comfortable.

Sally's assailant had the bearing of a person whose life was filled with short deadlines, a shorter fuse and even less love. She was the aunt from those films. The one no one wanted. She was made for this place. Barely a head above Sally, she was, nevertheless, towering in control. There was no consideration in the grip around Sally's arm. It was painful.

The corridor turned right. Sally thought she recognised the proportions of the corridors in an instant. Was she still in this awful building? As she was pulled around, Sally's hip twisted and her arm rotated backwards to freedom. She spun on the spot and started to accelerate. Her hair paused in the moment, to catch up with her head. There was no word. No sound. No pain. Her feet didn't move a step. In the moment of release, there was a new prison. Outside of the containment of her captor, she lost her ability to move.

A small part of the floor around her feet lifted up an inch and left her there, facing away from nobody's aunt. Her body had been neatly divided into two. The autonomic function remained: the brain and the organs ticked along nicely, thank you. The rest of her was immovable. The aunt might as well have flicked a switch and turned it all off. Sally continued to breathe, though. She felt the muscles around her lungs allowing air in and out. Sally whimpered a moment and, through it, reclaimed some hope. Sound meant voice. It wasn't a complete stop. She was leaning slightly forward. By all accounts, she should have fallen over, but she stood there, hanging upright.

"You can resist all you like," said the aunt, "but you will fight for Earth."

"Will I?"

"You will fight because that is what we require of your kind. There is no alternative."

"I'm looking forward to seeing how much firepower those little fighters have. I bet this place won't last long."

There was a pause from behind her. Sally wondered what the woman was doing. Was she laughing? Would Sally be shot down if she so much as looked at the building?

"I haven't even flown one of your stupid ships, anyway," Sally muttered.

"That's what you think," the aunt retorted.

The tile tilted suddenly under Sally's feet. Had she not been stuck, she would have fallen backwards, into a heap on the floor. Her body remained straight, despite the angle. Within a second, the aunt's arm was over her shoulder and tight against her neck. There was a touch of heat at the base of her skull. She could only tense up her jaw.

"What are you doing to me?"

Her captor didn't reply. Sally was released as suddenly as she was grabbed, and the tile elevated her back to vertical and rotated one-eighty degrees, until she was face-to-face with the aunt. The woman's eyes moved from side to side. Only an occasional blink marked the limit of her movements. No words, no sound.

"You might be right. Why are you right?" said the woman. She paused again. "According to the data link, you've had three weeks' instruction," she concluded. "What on earth did they teach you, if not flight school? You're tantamount to useless."

There was her mother's favourite word. Sally was ever desperate to prove it wrong. When her internal voice had taken up the reins, she felt the battle could not be won. She focused on the aunt's white knuckles. There was movement. A slight tensing and releasing of the muscles around the fingers and forearm. Was there something in her hand, communicating with her, perhaps by the sense of touch or telepathy? Sally thought back to when she and Jason had been captured by the guards.

Could the system be disrupted?

Sally blurted out a stream of questions. "What time is it? Does this building have any colours, other than white?"

The aunt's hair was slicked down. Sally's mind strayed back to what they had thought of as the basement of this strange building. Dimly lit corridors, moss or worse growing on the walls. There was that unpleasant squelching wherever she put her feet. She cringed at the memory of the sickly moisture seeping into her socks. This woman could have used whatever had been on that floor to keep her hair in place.

Sally's position wasn't uncomfortable. She was in no pain. She wasn't under any immediate stress, but she hadn't moved for several minutes. A treacherous thought scurried into her mind and told her she might never move again. The closest thing she could compare it to was being winded. She could breathe, but not deeply.

She should have been terrified, but her body wasn't responding. She was conscious and totally dependent. There was a squeeze on the crow's feet around her captor's eyes but, otherwise, no reaction was forthcoming. A realisation struck home.

"Wait, what instruction? What are you talking about?" Sally asked.

Colour returned to the woman's hand as it relaxed. A decision had been made.

"We shall go to the centre," declared the aunt, though Sally wondered if someone else was giving the orders.

The woman set off back the way they'd come. Initially, Sally thought she'd be left there and would, in time, have moss growing on her. When the woman passed her by a few feet, the tile rotated a half turn and moved in, behind her guardian. She was the duckling following its mother. They passed where Sally reckoned they'd exited her mocked-up bedroom. At the end of the shorter corridor, they turned left and faced a dead-end, a few paces away. Maybe it wasn't the same building, after all. That didn't make her feel much better. She wondered where Jason was.

The woman stood in front of her. Her hand could have twitched but Sally's tile was angled slightly up, so she couldn't be sure. The wall ahead of them silently swept past, as though the room on the other side of the wall inhaled. This room was all too familiar. The metal ball remained in its place hanging from an unseen link to the ceiling. Walls were full of information, broken into smaller parts. Most had data, some streamed pictures. To the right was a large screen in a grid made from red lines. There were numerous blue points at the lower end of the screen, around larger coloured balls on white trajectory lines. At the top there was a large green blob that appeared to flicker, fade and strengthen in equal measure. This screen would have covered the length of the wall but for the ball. There was a new addition in the middle of the room: a circular platform, one metre across. It was about an inch high and made from a reflective material.

Balls of blue light flowed from one side of the room to the other. As her tile moved into the room, Sally could see the balls contained words, numbers and pictures. Most cascaded into the circular platform. Some were sent back on the same path. Others moved between the men and women on the right side of the room.

Sally's tile merged into the floor as the aunt strode forward. Once the tile was absorbed into the ground, Sally's movement was restored and she half slumped in celebration. So relieved was she, she checked everything worked as it should do. Fingers and toes wiggled; she smiled, grimaced, frowned then shook her body in a kind of offbeat dance routine. Her heartbeat rose. The nervous system was catching up, after having been off duty for a while.

The aunt was standing near the platform in the centre of the room and her head was bowed. Sally was disinclined to follow and strayed towards the screens, on the wall to her left. Ninety percent of the data was given up to information on supplies, munitions and ships. Infrequently, the details on the screen condensed, circled and morphed themselves into a sphere. It pulled away from the screen and either went to another screen, or over to the reflective platform. One ball passed right through her head. The room went all blue and she ducked away. It travelled on. In that moment, she was aware of the information carried inside. All the goings on up there in high orbit.

After she separated from the orb, her thoughts were scrambled for a moment. Video links from different parts of space jumped from one screen to another. So many screens. She wondered how many people were up there. Surfaces were grey, except the control centres, where most of the people stood or pored over screens. Elsewhere, there was movement of personnel. Supplies flew through corridors and lift spaces. Lights flashed and sounds alerted the humans about food, new parts, personnel and more. They showed people in combat dress: uniforms, helmets and gloves. Insignia on the sleeves indicated the skill set and tasks. Panels sewn into lower sleeves indicated health status. Most flickered amber to denote a nervous anticipation but, in front of Sally, there were green lights across the board. It blurred with the detail. Too much to register.

How could anyone keep track of it all?

Two men on the other side of the room watched her between their tasks. They wore a smart-casual affair under their lab coats. On the upper pockets of the coats was the gold lettering 'TRP'. One man was older with a face for radio, yet he carried a smug bearing. He could lose himself in a crowd. His hand opened up and, in the space, appeared a ball that, aside from the colour, was empty. His other hand pointed at something on the wall and the ball then became a mass of information. He flexed his fingers and the ball lifted and moved up, then disappeared. His colleague made a catching gesture and possibly to Sally's eyes, the same ball appeared there. This was technology so advanced it appeared to her as magic. He could have been playing a game. It was a shame he looked as if he knew his actions outstripped her knowledge. He was showing off. The man's over-exaggerated movements were his own downfall.

He wouldn't be able to look cool even if he stepped out of a freezer.

The view changed to deep space. Between the systems, a large, green miasma was, even now, moving towards them. It filled her with a sense of dread. In spite of Sally's lack of interest in the man, he came over to her and delivered his assessment.

"They won't arrive too near our sun. But they won't arrive at the outskirts of the system, either. It's too far for them to manoeuvre, under normal power. They'll probably exit *H-space* in the spaces near the larger planets. Possibly outside the asteroid belt, if they're feeling brave."

A new screen began generating data and drew Sally's attention to the wall. It revealed an update of an evacuation. According to the available data, Earth's population was down by eighty percent. What fate had befallen them was not shared. She drew closer and saw a ship, lifting away through Earth's blue atmosphere. She touched a finger on the vessel and the earth disappeared off the edge of the screen, as the focus fell on the ship. It was in the same category of attractiveness as the man behind her. It wasn't ugly. It just wasn't worth her attention. It was a three-dimensional, black rectangle. No name, no shape, no bulges and no colour.

Was this designed during a power cut?

A design screen indicated it was modular. All ships in the same boring structure. Just bolt on the pieces you need, so long as all the lines are straight.

The ship vanished and the view pulled back enough to see it reappear, in the orbit of Jupiter. Not near the planet, but in its trajectory. There, it angled upwards, disappeared again and reappeared, away from the planets. Sally reminded herself that this was the gravity drive. The old established galactic power had seen Earth in the past and were amazed the population had made it into space. Somehow, those Earthers had stopped killing each other long enough to crawl up the evolutionary ladder. The Empire was certainly surprised when this supposedly backward planet leapfrogged them in space travel. Sally froze.

How do I know that? Just what is in my head? Did something happen when the ball passed through me?

She asked for details of the fleet. She saw a top-down view. Nestled in between battleships and cruisers sat the single-seat vessels. Fighters were positioned in groups in high-Earth orbit. Their keen-eyed pilots and keener-eyed systems watched and waited to be deployed.

"Zoom in," said Sally to the screen, but it registered no response.

She rattled through related words, including 'enhance' and 'magnify' but the screen ignored her. She pressed two fingers to the screen and moved them apart, tapped and double tapped, to no avail. Perhaps it was that woman in the wall – the entity Sally and Jason seen before, who powered all this technology – was all-powerful. Such a minor request, in the grand scheme of things, was never going to be acknowledged. Although it pained her to ask, she looked over at the uncool man and beckoned him over. He left his post with a smile and duly arrived, with the smuggest face imaginable. He placed all the fingers of one hand on the screen; he twisted it slightly, then rotated his hand away from the surface. The information spilled into his palm as a sphere.

Yes, of course. Why not? Sally thought.

"And how do you enlarge or reduce the view on the screen?"

Smugness was wiped off his face and replaced with doubt.

"No one's ever asked that." He tried to make out that it was a strange idea.

Not so smart.

"So," Sally continued, "how do we set it up to allow me to change the view, based on how my fingers move around the screen?"

The man became all frowny and his forehead wrinkled, until an answer was found. Then, released from his endurance, he scuttled back to the safety of his side of the room.

The information was conflicting. Earth's forces had had a good run and won most of the battles in which they took part. Yet here, they clustered round their home planet with a defensive plan. The Earth ships were notoriously small and underpowered. Hit and run – or, hit and run *off* – was all they were good for. Intelligence reported that there was confidence from the invaders. They were bringing everything to finish off the Earthers. Once the attacking fleet had prepped for intra-stellar travel, there would be little point in these humans turning up.

The Alliance fleet arrived, high above the orbiting line of planets but as close to the system as they dared. Tracker screens darkened as a huge surge in gravity compressed their arrival zone. As the enemy ships were released back into normal space, gravity released and upwards of twenty thousand vessels appeared. They far outnumbered the home team. After their jump, their energy systems were depleted and it would take time to recover before they began their attack. This was the time for the defenders to strike. Instead, they sat there, doing nothing.

The vast distances from one star system to another looked empty. In between lay astronomical minefields of unseen matter and energy. The longer a journey, the more a ship collected these dangers in their path. Collect too many and a ship might not make it. Earth's ships jumped smaller distances to detect and avoid such obstacles. First action on arrival to a system was to cleanse everything or they'd damage their ships. The newly arrived fleet remained unharmed as they detoxed their systems from inter-system dark energies. There were a few noticeable holes in their formation where interspatial anomalies had had the better of a few ships along the way.

They expected all Earth's vessels to be scattered around the system. It was believed that a mass exit from *gravity-drive* would terrify the defenders and leave them with a clear run to their little blue home, around their yellow star, Sol. However, they found no such separation of forces. This part of space was empty. There wasn't even a minefield, which had been a standard arrival gift in some quarters. Unbeknownst to most, ships waited in the shadows of Sol's system, including planetary moons and a few asteroids. Many dots were empty metal hulks – wrecks from other battles or buildings lifted and left in space. To the invaders, Earth had twice the quantity it had ever fielded. Both sides had trackers, but there was a sense of concealment. You might see a screen full of dots, but you really only trusted your eyes.

CHAPTER 2

Jason cast his eyes around the cockpit. The layout looked familiar. That was probably from the games he'd played with Mark. Everything was where he expected it to be, except him. He didn't want to be here.

The call had gone out. The frontline forces were making their way forward. He would be in the next wave. He waited for the completion of the pre-jump check. Would the seals on the cockpit window be strong enough against the vacuum of space? He'd find out soon enough.

Apprehension was high in his heart. With Earth below him, he joined other fighters and vessels readying to deploy. Thousands of ships littered his screen. A few of the alien ships were immense, he'd learned. He was to leave these for Earth's bigger ships.

The sky at night was full of pinpricks of light. As the blue atmosphere faded and became darker, he hoped to be surrounded by stars, comets and planets. It was full, but full of ships and fighters. Slabs and chunks of grey and black that were hard to pick out from the sky. A tracking console that was full of colour and, too often, warning sounds and flashes indicated something bigger. Occasionally, a higher priority vessel passed through his immediate space. He was warned it would do so, whether or not he moved out of the way. All the while, he was advised to proceed to certain coordinates, to join up with a squad of fighters. There was a sense of enforced excitement or an edginess that took his mind away from the sickening nerves. It had overshadowed his route from the building to here. As he saw all the other vessels, he hoped some of their pilots were feeling scared, too.

At home, there had been fighters and interceptors and bombers. Here, Earth's ships were all based on the same design. So far as he could see, all the other fighters were the same as his. No bombers or other specialist designs were visible. He didn't know if that was good or not. There was another beep. He was ordered to alter his route. Jason, halfway between fear and loneliness, did as he was told.

Earth wasn't shrinking as his fighter manoeuvred itself into the stream of other ships heading somewhere. *The Poseidon* was the ship that would carry him to the frontline. Him and the rest of the squadron he'd been assigned to. There were others around. It wasn't long before its captain signalled *jump* and Jason ran a final check. A heaviness squeezed against him from all sides. He wanted to clamp on his nose and clear his ears, but the helmet prevented him.

The compression escalated. Jason had to force up his visor to grip his nose between one thumb and forefinger. He ignored the cockpit warning about an insecure helmet. He breathed out gently to reduce the pressure on his sinuses. The forces continued to build beyond his ability to depressurise his ears. Just as he thought his brain might try and escape out through his ears, a whistling sound of air started. He pulled his hand away from his face and shut the visor. The distant stars blurred, melted and scrambled uncertainly towards him. Just as they were about to touch, they disappeared. Earth and the sun vanished, too. It all went dark. The cold touch of fear flared his nose, and cold air rushed down his neck and into his lungs. Electricity tingled in his back and arms. The surface of the cockpit reflected the lights of his display back at him, until they, too, faded and died. A moment ago, he had been surrounded by hundreds of ships and now, it was just him.

What have I done?

The compression remained. There was no way to tell if he was moving. His muscles began to buckle under the intensity, and it took all his effort to tense them. In a heartbeat, it all eased. Everything. The weight, the blackness, the ships. He could still feel a pressure on him, but he could breathe. He took short, sharp breaths in and out, as his eyes started to lose focus. Outside his cockpit, the black changed to a bright amber, as liquid fire poured on and over his ship. Other fighters appeared where they had been in formation, moments before. They were much more tightly packed in than they had been, before it went dark. One wrong move and it would be a pile-up. They, too, were being splashed with this curious fluid. Jason waved at one of them, for the comfort of acknowledgement. When it wasn't reciprocated, the loneliness returned.

He had the weight of the universe – or, more likely, this part of it – on his shoulders. His own movement met with resistance. He remembered swimming underwater, in the sea. Visibility was good until a wave crashed on top of him and clouded up the view. It was similar here but the waves were made from yellow and orange, with touches of blue as he sat in his own submarine. And there was no way to tell which way up was. It flowed from all directions. He was on the cusp between fear of the unknown and the excited frontier life of the adventurer.

The amber turned to fire, though still in a fluid form. Fire hurled itself against the window of his cockpit, then spilled away. It glowed with all the energy of the molten metal his ancestors poured into their moulds.

A second lurch and the pressure dropped like a stone. It removed the fire and amber and Jason returned to the blackness of space. Other fighters around him began to form up into a coordinated group. His rear-facing mirrors told him that, some distance behind, was a star. It looked larger than the ones on the veil of night, but smaller than the moon was from Earth. He wondered what it was called. The back of his head heated up and he knew how to activate *telemetry*. He smiled. It was *Sol*. A long way off, but still his home star. It had taken seconds to reach here. How long might it take to return under his own power?

The *Poseidon* landed between the orbital paths of Mars and Jupiter, though neither planet was in sight. A stream of battle-scarred fighters waited for a return journey. Some required repairs to the pilot, ship or both. Jason tried not to notice that some of the fighters were torn apart so badly, that it was unlikely anyone had survived. His head turned away but his treacherous eyes swivelled back.

After all the amber light and fire, the way ahead was that much harder to see. The *Poseidon* was obvious. There were at least eight other fighters he should have been near, but there was no sight of them. Over his earphones, he heard familiar voices. One advised to drop the cockpit tint back to clear, then automate the mirrored visor. The visor anticipated direction. If any of them found themselves about to face the sun, it would darken.

He rotated his vessel, though maintained the direction and low speed. Before, he'd seen Earth right underneath him. Now, there was only darkness and the nearby ships, including the *Poseidon*, didn't fill it up enough. He wanted to huddle against the larger ship for protection. Here, there was nothing to save him from the enormity of it all. It was all black on black – or black *in* black.

A moment ago, there had been no way to tell which way was up. Now, it was all down. Forward, backward, left, right. It didn't matter. There was only the emptiness. Nothing was nearby. He could see the sun, but it was so far away. If he became separated from his fighter, he could fall forever. Out there in the void.

Alone. His squadron were all around him but he still felt isolated. Voices came over the channel and they sounded so confident, so in control. When Jason's turn came to report, he reported all was green. He didn't add that the only green part of him was his stomach.

The squadron pulled away from the *Poseidon*. This was a group to which Jason had been attached but had never before met. He was with people he didn't know. Other fighters of his size gathered up around the big vessel. There was a build-up of light around the *Poseidon*, which expanded around the smaller fighters. When he thought he could look at it no more, the brightness disappeared and all of them were gone.

Chatter in his ears was a constant chaos and he couldn't turn it off. Beneath his awareness, information flowed through his helmet to an interface built into the base of his skull. He remembered how to prioritise broadcasts. Friend or foe communications were encrypted. He was not to follow orders unless they came with the correct authority. There were other instructions, but the display in his helmet issued a high priority message. They were to scout out this area for signs of the enemy. In this squad, he was *Lima Nine*. His task was to sit at the back and warn if the enemy approached from the rear.

A few asteroids drifted by. A large shadow was cast over them, and Jason turned his ship on the spot ninety degrees anticlockwise. A large asteroid rolled between them and the distant sun. To look at it, one would think Mars had heaved into view. However, the red planet was not to be seen. This asteroid was large enough to build a city on. It twisted lethargically between them and their arrival point. Soon, the temporary eclipse was over and the sunlight returned.

A tall, slim, glowing figure appeared in front of the aunt, who received an instruction, hesitated a moment, then sought out her former captive. The human in the conversation pointed at Sally, then down to the floor where they stood. Reluctantly, Sally approached.

As Sally drew near, she observed some feminine qualities in its blue face and shape. It was – or wanted to look like – a *she*. She offered a smile, but not one born from warmth. Sally wondered whether the blue lady had the power to affect her environment physically. Her smile was like an overpowering handshake. The aunt drew Sally's attention, then flicked a nervous glance back at the blue lady. The woman moved quickly enough to grab Sally by the arm and the back of the neck. She ducked, but could not avoid something being pressed on her neck.

Lady Blue was an unnerving sight. It – or *she* – was transparent and emanated a deep blue light. Not deep blue as in the atmosphere on a sunny day. This was more like a bruise. It could have been made from the same substance as the information bubbles. It appeared to be wearing clothes in the same colour.

Sally bent forward and cried out against the treatment. No amount of noise helped here. No one in this room was her friend. Was it the blue lady who was touching her? She couldn't stand up but couldn't see any other feet around. The back of her neck was touched in the same place as it had been in the corridor. While this, too, was a burning feeling, it was a cold one. Had the heat come from the human touch and the cold from the machine? The aunt held her firm.

A voice, not the aunt's, said, "I'm only after my memories. Once I have them back, you are free to leave. You are of no importance."

Jason's ship switched off. No light except for the distant stars. No sounds but his own breathing. He looked around. Leaned as far forward as he could. Twisted his head. The rest of *Lima* were apparently all struck by the same power loss. His first mission. His first engagement, and they were easy targets. He reached out and waved a hand through the power button once, then again, then repeatedly. All to no avail. Even the light on the inside of his helmet faded. Without the distracting light in his eyes, his irises widened, but there wasn't much to see.

He sat amongst the majesty of the stars. He was in a war zone and there should be no splendour to be had here. If he stood on the hill at home, he might see twenty miles. Here, he could see millions of light-years. Light was visible from the stars but they were a long way away. The sun was the only reference point but, with no power in his system, he didn't know where Earth was.

In the middle of nowhere, and from nowhere, came the nausea. When he left Earth and gathered with the other ships, the planet was beneath him. It was below him and down. Down meant there was an up. There was glass near his feet but, with the base of the cockpit in the way, he couldn't see down. He could see up, and there was a whole heap of nothing. No up and no down. A thought manifested itself and told him he was upside down. He had no means to challenge it. He did not wish to be surrounded on all sides by a hard vacuum, with a helmet full of his own vomit. He couldn't prove which way round he was; he tried to believe he was the right way up. He tried to relax his arms and noticed they fell to his lap. He raised them again, one at a time. Was that the engine or something else behind his seat? Whatever it was, it gave him a link to normality. It seemed, for the moment, there was at least a relative 'down'. The nausea took a turn and left the stage.

The sickness hadn't entirely departed. It was waiting in the wings, ready to be called upon at a moment's notice.

Ahead and to the right of him, some stars appeared and some disappeared. Something was moving. A thin streak of white traced a line then disappeared. After a few seconds, it reappeared. A comet? The shape in the gloom looked as large as the *Poseidon,* but circular. Not a sphere. A disc. If his computer had been on, it would have told him the species; the class of ship; where the guns were located; where best to aim to disable its engines or communications.

One of the other fighters passed Jason's within a few metres. With no stabilising power or any control, they moved on the last adjustment they had made. The incoming ship was a saucer but it didn't spin. As it approached, it turned on one axis and a whole side lit up. Not clean and pretty as he'd imagined, but it had slim lines of blue from the centre to the rim. There was a white line in between.

Jason estimated the rapidly decreasing distance between the approaching vessels and their solitary squadron. Rushing off to fight is a noble thought, when you're at home. When you and your foe are rushing towards each other, it's different. Each had sufficient tools to cause significant harm and distress to the other. He worried about losing a leg, his sight, his life – and they hadn't even fired a shot. In this powered-down state, he didn't think he was even going to have that choice.

Jason's hands began to sweat. Sensors picked up on his tension and the suit cooled in most areas. A whisper came through. It was quiet and fast. So fast, he thought the words went directly to his brain without bypassing his ears.

"One destroyer class. Twelve interceptors. Let them pass. Stealth protocol has been enforced."

If there was another function left to deactivate, Jason didn't know what it was. Then he did. He reached forward a finger for environmental control, and the air flow in his suit died. The sweat that had been defeated was free to make a comeback. All the background noise and distraction faded away; he could hear a faint rumble from the engines. They couldn't be totally deactivated because they would never be reactivated out here. And, should they be discovered, they might need to accelerate in a hurry. He kept his hands on his lap, in case he inadvertently turned something on, but they fidgeted. If the enemy detected him, they would undoubtedly award him a hearty *hello* and *goodbye* in a brief package of ordnance. Instead, his fighter drifted. However, he was at the business end of the guns of twelve other fighters, plus the destroyer. It made him long for the bare minimum of life-support in the form of cool air, but he feared turning it on. Sweat escaped his pores. He wasn't bathing in it but, even if he was, it would be a small price to pay for living.

The enemy closed in. Jason was certain they were near enough to start firing. Without any distractions, the noise from the engine was bothering him now. Was his ship quiet enough? Could the incoming vessels hear it? Would they pick him out then shoot at the squadron, all because of him? He should escape. Leave here and hope the enemy would chase him. The squad would be safe. Maybe. He wouldn't be. Not with twelve fighters and a ship firing at him.

His heart pounded and he wondered if they could hear it. The sweat flow went up a level. It was probably in fourth gear. He flexed the fingers of his right hand then didn't dare to touch the stick, placed against a console, in case he moved. He placed his hand on his right thigh, opposite the other one, in what he thought was a calm pose. It wasn't long before he scratched at his neck where it met the helmet, then scratched under his arms. Then he stopped, in case the approaching ships could see this.

Was the enemy waiting for the last second to unleash their assault? A short burst of energy from their weapons would do for him and much of his squadron.

And the award for the shortest time in combat goes to— played in his head, in various versions.

Then he pictured himself floating in space without his legs. Fifth gear anxiety was selected as his breath quickened. He hoped there wasn't a sixth. That the others in his squad could be experiencing the same didn't help as much as he hoped. It was true, they were the same team. He thought, if one of them flinched in this life-or-death game of *chicken*, all their numbers would be up.

The destroyer moved in with twelve triangular escorts. Jason held his breath and closed his eyes. He was afraid that, if he could see and hear things, the enemy might pick up on it. Without the control of sight, his thoughts raced. Out here, there was nothing to hide behind.

A loud thump scared the living daylights out of him. It came from above and he wrenched his startled eyes open to see another fighter, bouncing harmlessly away. He scanned the area to see what the enemy was doing. Jason was so caught up by what the ship might do to him, he didn't realise it had passed by. He glanced above him, inside his cockpit, to see in his rear-view mirrors and watched the retreating glow of their engines. He continued to wait. He didn't know when it would be a good time to start powering back up again.

Is it fate that I am sent to combat, only to sit quietly in a chair, sweating away? Death by dehydration, while drowning in sweat?

He was using line of sight to determine how far away they were. With a view based on the reflections of engines, he couldn't decide where the enemy was. He waited for direction from the others. Their lights had faded so much, he couldn't tell them apart from the stars.

He still couldn't see what function was where and requested a little light.

"Identify power options," he whispered.

He waved a finger at the relevant section. Energy systems powered themselves up slowly. No active radar as yet.

Let their signals come to you.

Little sparkles of energy appeared on his radar to denote the ships of his colleagues. Their energy levels eased up. *Lima* squadron had lost its form and were scattered, but not too wide. It would take only a few seconds to pull themselves back into a fighting force. He found he was still holding his breath and let it out, with great relief.

"How did that happen?" he queried, in a quiet voice.

'Psionics' appeared on the screen from someone as if that was enough to explain the turn of events. It didn't mean anything to Jason. Text was translated to sound.

Voices in his head reported that the destroyer was a scouting party. If it carried on, it would take a good few hours to reach Earth. By the time it arrived, there would be a substantial party of greeters. Another voice speculated it may have been drawn to this area by the appearance of the *Poseidon* and come looking for it.

"It can't be," countered another, "the rest of the fleet are too far away. This must be a specialist team. Scanning our defences."

"How so?" replied another.

Before anyone responded, a voice called, "Look out!"

The view blurred and Jason's ship was drawn forwards. He grabbed the manoeuvring stick, pulled it away to stop the movement, then a little further back to restore to his original position. He noticed the other fighters around him making corrections. As the squadron moved around him, two Earth destroyers appeared directly ahead. No designations appeared on his tracker but they were larger than the *Poseidon*. Maybe even half as large again. Their arrival released a wave of energy into the immediate space and Jason's eyes flickered to the mirrors and trackers. Dropping stones into a pond sent out ripples and alerted everyone nearby. The ships that had just passed them were indeed altering course.

Exclamations erupted from several sources at once. One voice in the newly arrived destroyer stated they had authority. The new ships engaged their engines and propelled themselves forward and ordered *Lima* to act as cover. The enemy ships had turned and were winding up their engines to full speed.

This was it. This was happening. The tension was back in spades. Jason didn't know where was best to go. Should he adjust his position in the squad to avoid the opening salvos? Tracker said ten seconds to firing range as both sides were rushing towards each other. Their destroyer would shave a millisecond from that. That's no time at all. *Lima* would have to work hard against their fighters and avoid the heavier weapons of the big ship. Otherwise, they would need no time to scatter *Lima's* ashes.

Five seconds. Jason's squad of nine had broken up into three groups of three: one to the right, one in the middle and his to the left. The two destroyers were above and below. Jason was confident his side would smash them.

Three seconds. Another large power surge from their two destroyers and they disappeared.

One second. Jason swore as his finger fumbled for the trigger.

They have no chance now.

♟♟♟♟♟♟

Sally staggered back, clutching the back of her neck with both hands and hugging the sides of her neck with her forearms.

"What? What is wrong with you?" she puffed out, caught between outrage and injury.

"Means to an end," was all the blue lady offered and then it faded into the floor.

Sally looked at the aunt who stared at her, then offered Sally only a scant few words.

"Reclaiming information."

Images in her head that had lain, undisturbed, were now released and brought forward for conscious attention.

I've seen these before. I haven't been here, but I've seen these before. How is that possible?

Images and scenes. Briefings and discussions behind closed doors. A particular face emerged in scene after scene.

A montage of memories released into her mind. Imagine being away from home for a year. When you returned, all your friends sent you updates at the same time. Images and sounds poured into to Sally's mind. No dates. No order. She stood still as her mind tried to find a pattern.

CHAPTER 3

Jason felt registered the betrayal as he pulled the trigger. The vessel responded with a prolonged salvo of fire. Jason fired first and metallic rounds scattered forward before they began striking the enemy, cracking hulls and knocking them fractionally off course.

"Bloody open fire!" he shouted and the other eight ships fired pulses of red energy.

The enemy responded with single lines of blue. One enemy vessel twisted away, but Jason followed it unerringly and fired until it lost power. It then continued in a straight line. Not knowing if it was good sign or a lie, Jason continued firing until the vessel broke apart. Only then did he let up and head to the next target.

Another fighter crossed his line of sight from his two o'clock, heading to eleven. In one movement, it stopped and went straight down, twisted and took a new direction. Jason twisted too, dropped the stick in his hand and fell in behind the enemy fighter. The movement squeezed him into one side of his chair then forced his stomach up. He straightened the stick and pushed it forward and set off after his target. He felt resistance from the back of the seat. A bigger, thicker blue line from behind filled the left field of his vision. He pulled away sharply, leaving the target, as the guns of the larger ship began firing in his area. He didn't fancy his chances against that weapon. Jason veered away at full speed. Instead, his team engaged the enemy's guns to protect their squadron.

"What about their fighters?" said a voice.

Jason didn't know the answer and pressed on. In his mirrors, he could see the other two, falling in behind as they made the points of a triangle. As he reached top speed, his two destroyers reappeared on the other side of the disc and began firing at it. The disc, caught between two lines of attack, froze for a moment, then turned its attention to the larger ships. Jason turned away, avoiding their weapons. Aside from his group, there were four fighters left on each side. He moved quickly to the scene, to add the extra vessels to tip the balance of power. Once engaged, the remaining four began burning more fuel to evade their pursuers.

There was a bright but short flash and a signal that the disc was dead. He managed a few shots to remove another enemy, then left the others in *Lima* to the rest. As they turned to look at the disc, it was missing a chunk of its hull and drifting, without power. Jason couldn't help but feel they should make sure. Yes, its hull was torn open, and there were bits floating out from it. He couldn't see any bits that might be life forms but he was travelling too fast to be sure. The enemy fighters had been flying away from him and he hadn't been able to see any crew there either.

Thoughts in his head scrambled to become audible and Jason asked why the destroyers left them.

"To confuse the enemy," came the abrupt reply.

The lead destroyer gave them instruction to target a new group of vessels.

"Time to intercept is under twenty minutes at full speed. We have other places to be. When you reach eighteen, we will return to add our power to the engagement."

The two larger ships moved forward. There was the familiar surge of mass and blurring of space; then they were gone.

Sally remained still as the new memories jostled in her mind. She found herself distracted by scenes of her, Jason and Simon. It was difficult to focus on ordering the flow of data.

Events from her timeline since she entered this building, on its various floors, corresponded with another. It could be those of the blue lady. One memory tried to overwrite the other. Sally saw it like a real memory and a daydream, on the same day, fighting for the same space in her brain. If the daydream won, would she be herself anymore?

Sally was confused by what she believed was the beginning. When she thought of that word, one memory said she and Jason climbed in through the window to avoid a man; a second memory opined it all started when Sally floated down to a floor, was herded out through the main entrance, brought back in then left in the foyer with Jason. Feelings intruded into her thoughts. At first it was a distant sense but, as she became aware of it, they strengthened with her focus. She felt malice and manipulation. Neither of these resonated with her. She filtered out these alternate thoughts by the feelings.

She glanced back at the screens and saw the large formation of attacking ships. Were they here to force a surrender, to seek reparations or to bring about the end of the world?

The last phrase triggered two concurrent memories. The first was her and Jason lying on that fabled bottom step seeing the destruction of everything. Everything but them and the stairs they perched on. The second memory was a discussion between the man with the grey streak in his hair and another. The man was looking at Sally in the image and she couldn't see who it was. It sounded like a woman. They'd said the scene wasn't real. The end of the world she and Jason had experienced wasn't real? What was the point of that? She wanted to know who the man was talking to. Her focus jumped to a position behind the man but most of the woman was obscured by him. Sally could see the woman's hair: shoulder-length, brown but no face. The man turned to look over his shoulder. This allowed Sally to see the woman's face.

"It's her," Sally recognised. One of the teachers from school. No, didn't she work in the office there? Was it a friend of her parents'? Someone else? Who was this woman?

Why did all her other thoughts lead to an answer except this one? Was she asking the right question? Be less specific.

When did she first learn of her? A memory arrived. Sally saw herself in an opened box. There were restraints to hold her in place. Wires connected her brain to a display. Lights pulsed along cables. Liquid food was fed into her body. The woman's face appeared on the wall next to her box. Sally saw her past self asleep so she wasn't meeting anyone here. Her attention was drawn to a display on the outside her box. It read, "Additional subroutine will trigger upon identification." There was a file linked that she tried to press. Nothing happened. This wasn't a daydream or her memory of being there. She could see herself in the box. These weren't her thoughts.

In the scene, a man moved between the viewer and the box she'd lain in. Sally could only see his greying brown hair. It was hard to see any clothes under his white coat. A hand reached out to the screen. There was no way for her to know who it was. Their finger pressed the error message. This revealed further details.

The man read the message out loud. "A flaw in the subroutine has led to an unforeseen outcome. The individual's memory pathways have been affected: additional data uploaded to the subconscious."

The memory darkened. Sally blinked and was back in the room. *What the hell was that?*

She knew her mind could wander off on its own. This was different. She'd never been there. But she'd seen herself, which didn't happen in dreams.

A cold feeling started in her nose and spread. By the time it had reached her arms and back, she'd pressed her fingers to her cheeks. *Have they done something to me?*

She shook her head. *There's no way. That sort of thing doesn't exist. How would you even insert a memory?*

The fog returned to her eyes and her attention was drawn away. When it cleared, she saw the same box. This time. She lay there in the box, her eyes closed, while two technicians plugged her into the machine. One technician faced her. He looked like he'd had too many early mornings, late nights and little time to eat in between. He was keen not to make eye contact.

The other one had her back to Sally. She occasionally turned her head to check the display. Sally watched impassively from a few yards back. When the pair completed their work, the man turned his face, but not his eyes, to Sally, in this moment, and spoke.

"All wired in, ma'am. Was there something you extra you wish for us?"

"This one is special. I would like to upload some additional information." To Sally it sounded like the words came from her but it wasn't her voice.

"From the training?" said the technician.

"No, from me." The unidentified voice sounded stern.

The technicians looked at each other. Both shrugged. The man continued. "What would you like to share with her?"

"I would like to learn how to upload data enough for her to recognise me at a later date."

The lady tech said something Sally couldn't hear.

"Turn to speak to me!" ordered the voice.

She turned slowly and looked in the same shape as her colleague. She delivered her comment with the same deference.

"Sorry, ma'am. I was starting to say that memories aren't compartmentalised. You could transfer additional data in the procedure. The training programme is focused. They learn what we want them to learn and no more. With the mind, even when digitised, cannot be controlled."

"You're exaggerating." Implied the speaker.

The lady glanced up and, for a brief moment, her green-brown eyes made contact. Then they widened and she looked away but continued.

"If you wanted to transfer a memory of your first flight in your vehicle, ma'am, you couldn't." The lady realised who she was talking to and continued quickly. "You couldn't just share it, that is. It would include your feelings, whether you felt nervous or happy, what you thought of the salesman, any other thoughts you had at the time and how you felt about them all."

There was a silence that lasted too long for the pair. The speaker ended it as their nervousness literally became nail-biting.

"Show me how to conduct the transfer and move to your next task."

Both nodded. The lady took her thumb from her teeth and took Sally's watching presence through the screens.

When the pair rushed away, Sally's character read information from the three-dimensional display. As the fog returned, Sally caught a glimpse of something that reached to interact with the data. She thought that it glowed blue as the fog overwhelmed her view.

Sally emerged back into the room with her hands pressed against her head. The cold feeling permeated every cell in her body. A tear welled up in an eye but she dabbed it out immediately. *Oh my God! What the hell was it all for? Why? Just why?*

More memories invaded her attention. These were familiar but still weren't hers. The briefing to the teams on the stairs, the green tubes. Each time, she remembered where she was when those images had first come to her.

⁂

Five minutes gone. Once they applied thrust in their direction, engines were switched to minimum. There was no resistance to slow them, so Jason fired his manoeuvring thrusters and rotated to look around. If the other six members of the squad were bothered by these antics, they didn't say. He was prepared to defend his actions by saying he was checking the rear. It was better than relying on the tracker and those small mirrors.

The planets this far out from the sun were the largest in the solar system. It was a disappointment that there was nothing to see. What joy it would have been to have seen Jupiter's red spot, up close. All that was visible from here was the sun. As it came into view, his visor darkened a shade. Of Earth, there was nothing to report. If it was in front of him, it wasn't obvious. He looked left, right, up and down. Then he stopped thinking that way, lest the nausea return. He tried to imagine what this was like but there wasn't a comparison. He had left his comfort zone far behind. Being perched on the edge of a cliff, looking down on to a beach might equate to this. If you were very generous about the size of the cliff. But, on a cliff, the beach or the sea would focus your eyes. Here, you could fall forever. Long enough to exceed anyone's lifespan. He pushed himself back in to the seat as far as he could go and turned to look back at the squadron. They offered him a stable reference.

Jason noticed a crack in his screen. It could have been from the combat, or when the fighter bounced off him when they were drifting. It didn't appear to be getting any longer or wider. It was simply there. His neck warmed up and he looked for *automatic repairs*. That system had been turned off when they went into stealth. It hadn't been a priority to reactivate. He pressed it, and a button flickered amber, for a few seconds. The crack took seconds to reseal. The light flickered long enough to make him worry what else was wrong. Then it went green and turned off. He shared this with *Lima* and received two positive messages back.

Ten minutes gone. He was elated to have survived. The loss of the two squadron members pulled him back down. He had been scared – terrified, even – when his little fighter had shut down, shortly after arriving here. He thought about that and he looked back at the smallness of the sun.

Where *was* home? Where did he need to get to where he could feel safe? More heat led to a scrabble of fingers in the space above the panel. Functions were visible, either on his visor or in the cockpit. Cycling through the information section, he found a map of the solar system. There was an occasional flicker but it was virtually the same display he had on his bedroom wall. Starting from the left was the sun then all the planets, not to scale, heading to the right.

"No," he explained, to whoever might be listening. "I want to see them in their current positions. Not all lined up."

The view changed. It realigned with the sun in the middle. Mercury was close in at twelve o'clock. Venus was slightly further out, at five o'clock. Earth was at three, then Mars and Jupiter were on the other side of the clock. Faint arcs extended a little way from each of the planets, indicating their orbits. The other planets didn't fit into his view.

There was a blue dot near the edge, at three thirty or, maybe, four. He reached out to it and it zoomed in, to show his little squadron of fighters. They might as well have been in deep space. For a moment, he wondered where Sally was. He looked in the direction of where Earth might be.

I hope she's okay, he thought.

He wondered if she had signed up too. Was there a way to find out?

Five minutes to go. Jason had dismissed the telemetric data and was hunting through other choices. A couple of selections on a sub-menu and seven small squares appeared in front of him. On each square he could see the shoulders up to the top of the helmets of, presumably, other members in *Lima*, as they piloted their ships. He could hear them, too. Jason spotted another option: covered or uncovered, so he toggled the latter. The helmets shimmered and faded, leaving just the faces. He was immediately drawn to his own face on the bottom row. He rolled his eyes and scrunched up his lips and nose and the picture updated, after a short delay.

Sticking his tongue out amused for a few seconds, until he looked at the others. He hadn't really looked properly, when they'd appeared. They were all young. Senior school-age, maybe. He wasn't familiar with faces but two of the men could be European. Two were women who looked African but sounded like they were born on his street but that could be due to the translator.

The last two helmets were strange. They had faded to reveal nothing. He toggled back and forth to confirm he hadn't made a mistake. Were they even his squadron? The two empty fighters were in his group of three. Had they died? Was it better to show an empty seat, rather than a dead person? But why were all ships flying as if they had pilots? Perhaps they were elite forces, invisible to such views for their own protection.

Four minutes to go. There was no movement or expression in the faces of the four. They had all just been in a fight and weren't far away from being in another. No looking around the cockpit. No checking instruments. They stared directly ahead.

Jason found a timeline option and changed the viewing point

back to the start of the engagement. He saw his own face flinching as each shot was fired at him. His head bobbed and weaved, as if that was going to make a difference. He had thrown up a hand to protect himself as the cockpit lit up from a nearby explosion. While he flinched and cowered and weaved, the others remained still and blank. The empty fighters made him feel uncomfortable, but not as much as the empty faces. He pressed the view button again. Pipes were going into their mouths and noses. A green fluid went in and a green fluid came out.

Jason's display indicated the time was down to less than three minutes and he turned his fighter to face their direction of travel. Energy levels for engine and munitions sixty three percent. They were a long way from refuelling. There was a power surge from the approaching enemy ships, ahead. Their communications channels were alive with energy.

Sixty seconds. The tracker said green, which meant the enemy, but these were big ships. Shouldn't they have fired by now? The sense of anticipation drove his adrenaline up. He looked around for some kind of help.

Thirty seconds. *Where were those destroyers?*

It felt oddly quiet as they approached the ships. They were better than these oddly-shaped constructs, with aerials and extensions stuck on in an ad hoc way. None of them were shooting. His squad, too, were holding back.

He dodged a few ships, then saw one nearby that looked, for all the galaxy, to be encased in glass. Seven spheres of transparent material, all were large enough to contain their own shopping centre. Each stuck out from a tubular stem, from which all the pods extended. There was a small cockpit at one end plus a huge block, which contained the engines. The contents were largely red. The computer analysis identified this as agricultural plants, for a planet with a ruddy atmosphere.

That's cheating. You can't bring a farm to a battle.

A message lit up in front of Jason's eyes. It was from command, asking *Lima* what the hell they thought they were doing. The two destroyers had been waylaid. They were to fire on the ships, immediately.

Jason confirmed the instruction, pushed up his speed and broke off, in his group of three. Eyeing up the farm pods, he sped towards the ship. On the final approach, he cut forward thrust and rotated his ship so it slid past the enemy. He fired at a pod whenever it came into sight. Other ships in his squad – led by his example, if not his exact technique – began firing.

Jason selected *energy attack*, more from curiosity than any plan. Balls of red released from his fighter and hit the pods, but caused no obvious damage. On his second pass, he switched back to the hard stuff, whereupon the glassy material shattered. The release of the atmospheric within, tore more glass away. The exhalation of air from the pods pushed the vessel away. It drifted dangerously close to another odd-looking vessel, which had to change course to avoid collision.

One of the other fighters swept low over it and released a bright, pulsing ball of light. Something in the back of Jason's head reminded him. It disrupted systems, caused power surges and blackouts. It struck the rear of the ship. The engine fluctuated for a while, before cutting out. Power failures occurred across the vessel and it began to drift. Jason found another likely target. He switched back to energy, held the button down for longer. When he released it, his own bomb descended into it. It missed what he'd been aiming at but still hit the ship. A voice came through in his helmet and told him not to worry.

"You can't really miss with these weapons. Your shot landed near the main power management area. Now the power is flowing in too fast for it to process and it will overload."

Sure enough, explosions occurred one after another where his shot had hit. His energy settings had declined significantly.

The two destroyers reappeared, swept in and made swift work of the remaining ships. The remaining fighters were ordered to arrange themselves into a tighter formation. The destroyers would take them to their next target.

CHAPTER 4

The face under the streak of grey looked back from the mirror. Knight had lived many lives to reach this point. Forward and back in time to make sure everything worked out. This final day had arrived. The threads of the known options of the past would become a single, unchangeable, unknown future path. Mistakes now could not be undone. His time had come. He would see the last hours from the place that had made it all possible.

♟♟♚♚♟♟

There was a new figure in the room. Sally hadn't seen all the comings and goings, but this one appeared. She'd scanned the room one way then back again. One moment, the blue woman was by herself and the next, he was in front of her. Sally recognised him immediately but couldn't name him. A face of inconsistencies, old features entwined with new. And, like the smug technician, the new man fancied himself just a bit too much. His scalp was balding, while his scant facial hair was going grey on one side. He wore dark coloured trousers, a white shirt and a dark waistcoat. As he walked, nothing he wore moved as it should. Something in her combined memories told her his name was Knight. *Have I met and forgotten him?*

Knight bowed his head to the lady, she nodded and spoke. Three yards around them, ceiling and floor reached towards each other to create a private room. To Sally's eyes, random images appeared on the outer walls, but no sound escaped.

Annoyed at not being able to listen in, she turned her attention to the screens. Sally was lost in the numbers, footage and communications. All the while, she was sorting and filtering out the images released into her consciousness. She was startled when a man spoke directly behind her. She turned to see it was Knight.

"They are probing us," he said.

There was only him. Lady Blue wasn't to be found.

Is he talking to me? Sally thought.

He looked directly at her and left her in no doubt.

"All our brave forces going to fight, and you're here," he sneered.

"Is it my battle?" Sally asked, trying to maintain confident eye contact.

"Alien forces are coming to destroy the Earth. I am wondering why you think you have been allowed the luxury of the choice to remain behind?"

I don't see you fighting, either, thought Sally, sourly.

She didn't express this out loud, believing it would have had no impact on him. She didn't think he was really interested in what she said or did. One more fighter up there wouldn't make a difference, especially given the casualty rates.

She turned back to the screen. *What is going on here?*

Let's start with an easy one, she thought, trying to change the subject from herself.

"Who is who?"

"Blue is us. Green is them. Blue because the Earth is blue, of course."

Sally let that go. By the tone of his voice, the colour had probably been his choice.

"That's one big blob of green."

"Yes, they are here. We have been waiting for them, before the first shot was fired."

"Do you know you're talking out loud?"

Sally regretted saying it as soon as it was out. She had no idea what he was capable of. She was more grateful that no memory had rushed forward to inform her. She felt his eyes on her for a long second before he continued.

"We invented this technology, of course."

There was the royal 'we' again. Everyone on the planet, in fact, had a part in inventing this technology. If he spoke long enough, he might claim he'd invented fire and the wheel, too. There was a pause, during which Sally presumed she was being invited to comment on his masterly strategy. She opted for silence. He didn't wait long.

"It's faster and, as green team are about to find out, usable inside solar systems," he continued. "Their big ships can jump huge distances in one go, but deep space has many dark and mysterious complications. Imagine flying through a mountain range at night without radar or lights. Utterly reckless. Our ships can better navigate the smaller turns, and it leaves less of a tear in the gravitation fields."

Sally didn't know what he was on about but nodded slowly. She recalled the 'Yes, dear,' her parents used against each other.

Knight managed to look aloof before he turned away to show his back to her, as if he thought she cared. Silence reigned before Sally, still piecing together the puzzle of images, made a connection.

"Perhaps they are coming because you invited them. Maybe they're karma in the form of an invasion and have come to undo your evil," she said, goading him.

Knight launched into a spiel.

"Humanity had reached up to the stars. It was almost

profound. However, team blue had been turned back by the species already there. Those early humans had the patience of saints."

Sally couldn't tell if he was quoting from a history documentary or the marketing brochure.

"Now," he added, "our brave people will take back what is rightly ours."

♟♟♟♟♟♟

Jason's ears popped as his ship was released back into what he decided to call 'normal' space. There were no green ships on his screens. He hadn't been flying much more than an hour but he was learning fast. His power systems, weapons and repair systems were up in the ninety percentages.

"How are all my systems back up?" he spoke, aloud.

"Larger vessels can transfer energy," replied a voice over his headset. "Just pray that it doesn't happen the other way round."

More chatter ensued from expressionless faces. There was energy in their voices but, beyond their lips, there was nothing. They weren't being instructed to go anywhere.

"There's nothing here. Why have we been brought here?" Jason asked.

"Taking a break. There are no other formations small enough for us to put a dent in without losing all of you. So, we wait."

The local chatter went quiet and Jason returned to his hunt for Sally among the channels. With so many forces spread across the solar system, there was no way to know where she might be. His initial efforts to put up all the faces on one screen resulted in pictures but they were too small to identify whether the seats were filled, let alone the gender of the occupants. He asked the computer to find any female pilots. Again, the results were too numerous.

"Young women? Girls?" he clarified.

"Please specify an age range," replied the automated voice.

When he did, he received no results.

♙♟♜♜♟♙

"Lies!" Sally blurted at Knight. "Your brave humans? They're all running away. How many of them are even up there? Tell me more about this grand evacuation."

Knight allowed himself to be distracted by a single engagement that soaked up a large number of resources. A box counted up two columns of losses in blue and green that Sally presumed corresponded to each side. When he spoke again, his voice was reverent with the righteousness of his cause. "Few wanted to fight and who could blame them? So, we issued an ultimatum: fight or flight. Most left."

"They all decided to leave?"

"Most of them. Funny thing, location. You grow up in a place and it becomes familiar. You know the rules. People learn to take it easy. Find yourself in another place, however, and the uncertainty returns, even if the rules are the same. You have to start over. Humanity reached the stars, experienced the best of advanced technologies across the galaxy, and became contented. Those that have made it to the new world are out of their comfort zones, possibly for the first time. They have discovered resources they never knew they had. The Alliance made us all soft and weak."

"Slaves," said Sally suddenly. "They're all slaves. You brushed over it by labelling them merely as 'others' but that's what they are."

From Knight, there came no sound.

"And the worst of it is," continued Sally, "they don't even know it."

♟♟♟♟♟♟

Voices came and went but Jason didn't recognise any of them. They'd been static for seven minutes and he was feeling like a bit of a fraud. Yes, he'd seen combat. Two engagements, already. One of them had been scary and they had lost two from his squad. The other had been against unarmed ships and shooting them up hadn't felt right. He would agree with anyone that not being shot at was a good thing. But shooting people who couldn't shoot back wasn't fair.

Eight minutes. Jason kept looking at his watch. He hadn't been able to relax. The destroyers could appear without even a moment's notice.

On the channels, there had been lots of shouting, screaming, and then sudden silences. The noise came through unfiltered and undirected. There was no way to identify the location of the action, only that it was happening. Fighting was intensifying. There were normal exchanges in between. He hadn't yet found an easy way to shuffle between squad chatter. Sometimes the communications system changed when there were no voices left to be heard. It wasn't helping him find Sally except, sadly, by process of elimination. The enemy were making shorter work of Earth's fighters in this battle. That wasn't a good thought. People were dying. He hoped she wasn't one of them. He hoped no one would die but it wasn't his choice.

Nine minutes. Another squad in another situation. *Shark* team had been talking about their successes in the war to date. They were on approach to a single Alliance vessel with a long beam and little thickness. It had rounded edges front and back, like a silver cigar. One squadron pundit was convinced their objective would soon be smoking. This was followed by a whirlwind of banter that made Jason so happy he fired up their faces to see who was saying what.

Nine pictures in a three-by-three block appeared in front of him. When they spoke, their pictures brightened. These faces were animated. There was life behind their eyes. They were older than his team. A couple of them looked older than his dad, and it was those two who were making most of the comments. There was none of the *short, back and sides* requirement for hair. The oldest man in the group had grown his brown hair to shoulder level. Once their target was picked out, side talk was side-lined.

Of the three women in the squadron, the one with the shortest hair observed, "No fighter cover."

The oldest man confirmed, "Noted. Increase to full and spread out in case of area effect. Aim for critical functions to disable, then on to our rendezvous with the *Vostok*."

The closer they headed towards engagement, the less they moved. Their eyes were twitching a little. He wondered if all the information they needed was being channelled into their visors. The conversational tone stopped but a certain confidence remained in their faces.

Jason overlaid a visual of their approach onto their faces. There was no explosion from an area effect weapon. There was no sound. One of them observed a power surge. Their cockpits were suddenly bathed in green light. Eyes went wide, frantic, terrified. Telemetry indicated to Jason they were all trying to escape with full burn. Then came the screams. Hands reached to faces but their helmets must have been in the way. Facial hair appeared and rapidly accelerated, hair extended and grey erupted from the top of their heads and flowed down to the ends of the hair. They all escaped the green, but the ageing continued. *If you're on fire, leaving the flames won't stop the burning.* Hair fell out, faces turned grey, skin lengthened and sagged. Voices weakened, as vocal cords aged. Stomachs upturned and threw out contents as far as the visor and was then forced back into mouths, still screaming. A few choked. By now, over half of them were dead. A few screamed on but, within seconds, they too were gone. But that didn't stop the effects. Within a minute, there was nothing but bones. There were no more screams except Jason's.

Jason's screams broke down into a sob, with periodic cries of "What the hell?" The acidic burn of his stomach reached his mouth and he stopped himself from throwing up. As much as he wanted to spit, he forced the bile back down with a hard swallow. A pipe made itself available inside his helmet and water was quickly delivered. He swirled it round his mouth to clear as much of the taste as he could.

He reached for the communications panel, turned off the pictures and returned to *Lima* radio. It was quiet but not blissfully so. He needed to hear the voices of normality but no one was talking. There was nothing to drown out the faces of *Shark* and he hoped it had been some mistake.

He spent each passing second fighting his own battle against being sick inside his helmet. He glanced at his watch. Thirteen minutes. He was still feeling sick when the two destroyers arrived, a minute later. He wondered how much water was left in the tube.

The captain of the destroyer issued his orders.

"Form up around my ship and be ready to jump."

While the ships aligned themselves, Jason asked, "Do you know about the green light that struck the *Sharks*."

"Watch out for green fields," came the brief and unhelpful response from the captain. "They appear in front of you in a mist. Not as clear as a ship or a fighter. Only a few enemy ships have this capability. They'll kill you within minutes – seconds, if you're lucky."

And that was that. Just a short piece that could have been delivered by Sally's mother: 'Don't touch this or that. Don't go in there. It's not for you.'

Yellow liquid splashed on the surface of his cockpit as they jumped to another part of space. There was something beyond the yellow. Something dark, but he couldn't make it out. One jump ended and another began. The sense of pressure pulled him down. His stomach rebelled and, once again, there was the bitter taste in his mouth. It took almost all his focus to stay on top of it. His ship began to shake.

A voice sounded in his ears. "Repeat, *Lima Seven*, you're too close. Check your position."

In a corner of his helmet display, 'L7' said it was him. He'd strayed too close to the destroyer. Ripples of energy were extending from its hull, causing tremors in his ship. More urgent instruction. Ripples became waves. One crashed on his ship as a yellow shot surged towards the front of his fighter. His breathing quickened. He gripped the stick but fear gripped him tighter. His movements lost their subtlety and he dodged the wrong way. He glanced off the destroyer then tumbled away. His racing heart pounded in his head. He couldn't stabilise his course. Another crack appeared in the screen and it split all the way down to his foot. Unable to regain control, he spun away. As he left the sphere of influence of the destroyer, he was shunted out into 'normal' space. *I don't want to die. I don't want to die.* The sudden change in gravitational effect tore at the crack on his screen as he tumbled out of control.

♙♞♝♝♝♜

Knight's confidence was unshakeable. Sally's awareness didn't seem to bother him. She interpreted this as an indication of her credibility or, worryingly, her life-expectancy.

What happens to those who know this much?

"Easy question for you. Who writes history?" asked Knight. He didn't wait for an answer. "In large numbers, people are a complication. Medical advances meant we either had to improve our game or focus our efforts, elsewhere. The population from your time to the arrival of safe, breathable air, dropped by four billion. That's more than enough to fight a war on many fronts."

Sally thought of the community on the hill they had stayed in. And they were a community. Things hadn't gone well but they lived and worked together. She remembered their food, the clothes they'd made and their weapons. It was all organised. The wife of the chief made it all happen and the chief gave the final stamp. She remembered so much about them. What she didn't know was what had attacked them in the night. This triggered a memory through the eyes of another. A night-time view approaching the settlement on the hill from above ground. An agent of *The Project* had targeted the village. An airborne assailant in stealth. The guards stood as much chance as a whale defending itself from a harpoon. She watched as the heavy wooden door yielded to pressure applied by a handheld device. The effect stunned the guards. The amount of force required to break that door should have woken people miles away but there was no sound. She saw a room full of sleeping people and one person looking at the fallen doors. It was her. She was sitting upright, mouth wide open. She saw now what she hadn't before. A weapon being pointed at her. It discharged.

"You shot me! Why did you shoot me?" she demanded.

"According to the report, you were the only one awake, in there. You knew something was amiss and began to shout. Luckily, our operative made a judgement call. You're alive. What's the complaint?"

"Jason said you took two children away. Their families think they're dead."

"They are all dead."

"What?"

"It happened tens of millennia ago. They are all dead. Life was short, back then. Unforgiving, even. They have lived longer here."

Sally's anger crunched up several gears.

"A life in green tubes. A few weeks in a claustrophobic container. How long up there before they're killed in a war you had no right to drag them into? How many millions did you kill?"

"Overall, we nudged up the mortality rate by a fraction of a percent. Hardly worth noticing."

"*Wow*. Does that make you feel all warm inside? Tell me, how many people is that?"

Knight looked away, smiled and looked back, meeting Sally's eyes without shame.

"Enough to defend the planet against the largest fleet ever gathered in one place."

"A war you started."

"It was inevitable."

"You took them from their homes. You destroyed their lives, their families. You created a war then trooped off to find someone else to fight it."

"Their lives were meaningless."

"Not for them. And meaningless compared to what? Decades, of their lives with their families, with everything they've know. All that compared to a short time of accelerated growth in a green tank and minutes of brutal fighting?"

"Dying in defence of the planet rather than defence of their community. The stakes here are somewhat higher and more meaningful. Go on, judge me with your eyes and your millennia-old temperament but most of these people would have fallen in a war, cut down in their prime by an axe, spear, arrow, rifle or gas. Is this better? It's no worse. How many died under the hooves of the Mongols, the trenches or the gas chambers? Is that your 'better life'? Was that more beneficial to the planet?"

His voice suggested he had not lost his cool but his eyes looked through her.

Is this guy for real? He had access to possibly the greatest tool humanity ever discovered. The ability to go forward and back in time. They could have made the world a better place. They could have stopped all the things he'd just listed. They could have spared billions and taken us to the stars so much sooner. We could have had long, happy lives filled with wonder. Instead, they delivered pollution, death, disease, destruction for all but a few. We barely have time to appreciate our lives then these idiots decided to shorten it.

Sally was flummoxed. Was it arrogance or ignorance that limited them to this outcome? Fighting was what you did when you ran out of options. He has no excuse for challenging past atrocities. She stared back into his burning eyes. *He's got to know, hasn't he?*

"How many people have to die for you? How much blood is enough? How many poor and starving? You compare civilisations based on their destruction but what about what was built, created? What of art and music and living?"

"Those populations you're talking about. They're not people anymore. Not really."

"There's a war on. You started it. You brought this on yourself. But you weren't happy with that so you dragged millions of others from other times into it."

"I'm glad you have all the answers. If you have any more, please bear in mind some of the other acts of the Alliance. One of their ideas was to destroy the larger planets in our solar system. Their aim? Who knows? One potential effect would likely have caused the Earth to change its orbit."

"Is that how you're justifying your actions? You're the bully in the playground. Now you're upset because some other kid has dared to hit you back. You started this. They're responding to your aggression. That's about as smart as attacking the sea because a wave made your feet wet."

When Sally stopped, Knight was gone but not only him. Everyone had left: the blue lady, the technicians and the bad aunt were gone too. Sally stood alone in the room. *Was that it? She figured it out and they leave?*

Her heart was thumping away. Her skin charged up in the exchange. Sally tried to get her breathing under control. It fluctuated as she thought of more things to throw at these idiots. *They'd made people survive the birthing process more easily, given them more children then taken them away. How many were taken?* The fog glazed in her attention but she recognised it and shook her head vigorously.

"I don't want to know." She shouted at the empty room. The fog faded away.

The screens were blank too. The only constant was that metal ball. Was this real? Was this another imagined scene where she'd been tested to see how she'd respond?

The scene from the settlement came back to her. It reminded her that Jason had been asleep beside her. She wanted to know where he was but was afraid to ask. She hoped he was somewhere safe. She wondered if she could find out.

CHAPTER 5

Far from anywhere and anyone, Jason sat in his fighter. Bright lights dominated his view: in the distance they were stars; in the middle distance, the brief flares were explosions in the battle for his home planet; in front of him, his consoles flashed warning colours of problems that needed to be fixed. He tried to push the thought from his mind that each of those flashes in the middle distance meant lives lost. He looked around for the next fight but he realised there wasn't one. Or, rather, there wasn't *just* one. It wasn't a single game. There were boards on top of boards and it was hard to see what was happening.

He looked at his broken fighter. Each side of the divide had bent away from the other. The cockpit, from where he watched, was no longer sealed. The eggshell had cracked. He hadn't felt a rush of air when it opened. His suit had tightened against his skin and created an airtight link to the helmet. When he moved, the suit resisted that part of his body. The unplanned exit during the jump had siphoned off most of his ship's power.

He was one person, one fighter, in the grand scheme of a battle. Who was going to come and rescue him? Who would come back for the pilot who couldn't fly straight? There was no earthly reason that anyone would waste the resources to pick him up. What if the other side found him? Would that be better or worse?

He soon started to notice the cold. The nausea hadn't gone away but, with the hole in his own fighter, there was no opportunity to open the visor and spit or cough his mouth clear. The vacuum would take more than the contents of his lungs.

A new explosion tore out the bottom left of his foot-well around the crack, taking more of the hull with it. Screen and metal fragments drove into the cockpit around him. He didn't feel the impact of the numerous shards as they danced off his suit and helmet, though he still flinched in panic. His fighter had been intersected by small rounds. A further shower of glass sped into the cockpit, bouncing over seat, suit and screen. Without air in the cockpit, he only sound came from shards of his cockpit screen striking his helmet. It came without warning. It could happen again.

The cold set in. He was losing feeling in his fingers. The gaping hole in front of him drained his confidence about survival. About life. About decisions. Keeping the body core warm was the priority. Maintaining control was becoming more challenging.

"What am I doing here?" Jason cried out.

It was Mark. It had been fine playing games with him for a while. Then Mark had left to fight a war. Jason had put on this stupid oversized outfit. He'd reluctantly clambered into this fighter. And here he was. In the middle of nowhere. Alone. He'd rushed off again. Not exactly rushed. He'd resisted in spirit but not in body and what good had that done?

It was his mum. Mark's and his that clinched it. He'd felt a connection and then a pressure to come. He hadn't wanted to. There was a war, a battle. He'd only seen it on that wall once. This wasn't his fight. He should have been in his room now. Except, his room, at home, opened onto a landing. This one had opened to a room with spacesuits and helmets. He was marshalled from one door to another by a woman who had half the height of Sally's mum but twice the attitude.

His brain hadn't been his friend earlier. If he'd had time to think. If only... If Sally had been with him. They'd worked well as a team. She'd saved him from the guards. Without her, he'd have been shot. Then what would have happened? He didn't know what could have awaited him. Like being lost in the middle of nowhere, he'd have been lost in a time not his own. It was like this, just like this. If he had been shot, what would have happened to Sally? Would she have gotten away? On the stairs, she'd figured it out. Would she have been able to climb in alone? Perhaps, but there was that ball as well. It had taken both their efforts to get passed it. What if she'd been the one to be struck by the cold? The chief would have found her.

They could have been taken off the site but to what end? They would have been in an alien world. Earth but in the future. People always want to see the future. He'd have been in it. A different time with different rules. No family, no friends; maybe Sally with him and both them thinking of the day he'd gotten shot and how they might have escaped.

He needed her. He hadn't realised how much till now. Alone and cold without her. He'd thought there was just a physical attraction but he felt a genuine admiration for her. When he'd thought he was saving her, she'd saved him. She'd formulated a plan to escape burning building and put herself in the way of harm for him. The fire had been too hot where he was. It must have been hell for her.

As much as he'd hated it at the time, he wished he could be there now. Better the fire than this cold. His suit was sparing him from some of it but how long would it hold? At some point, he would freeze. He would die.

She'd helped him and they'd escaped by going down another level. He hadn't reciprocated after escaping the fort on the hill. They weren't under pressure when they'd made it into the building. He had wanted her to recover as much as possible. Was it a mistake to have left before Sally was ready?

What was different now? His memories of his mum seemed fresher. Images forgotten were there, clear like they'd never been away.

Jason believed he was going to die out here. The weapons fire that tore his screen away showed him that much. He was vulnerable. He hadn't seen the ordnance coming. It was likely more could come his way. It was likely, he wouldn't see that coming either. If the same shells had come straight at him rather than from the side, they would have finished him. He wanted to hide someplace but there was nowhere to go. No place was safe.

His eyes welled up as he knew there was no escape. Tears released and poured down his cheeks. He turned this way and that but there was no escape from this truth. He could be a blink away from death. How long could he keep open his flowing eyes? He might never know what would kill him. In this time of desperation, he hoped for death in old age. Would he be that lucky?

He'd killed and others had been killed around him. For what? What was this doing for him? A cold, harsh memory pulled at him.

"What," he asked out loud, "was any of this doing for Simon?" He felt an anger inside. One that he couldn't quench. He'd wanted to help Simon. *How well was that going?*

Jason set a course for Earth and set his thrusters to whatever full speed was available. It could take hours, maybe days but at least he was going the right way.

♙♟♟♟♟♙

The adults had returned from where, they did not say. Sally was annoyed she had to ask their permission to go to the bathroom.

She couldn't leave the room without someone's say so. Yes, they were adults but they were hardly the ones she was used to. She might not like her parents but they weren't trying to kill her. Presumably she was under a surveillance she couldn't see. She hoped Jason had found a place to hide.

When she returned to the room, Knight was soon talking. She began to think he was distracting her from something or, perhaps, leading her towards it.

Hindsight is a wonderful gift and, if you can travel in time, you can avoid your troubles. The Restoration Project had become powerful with this technique. Powerful enough to take control and start a war. All the events that had led to now, could be influenced by returning to the past. From there, they give detailed instruction on how to respond. It worried her a lot that she didn't have to ask to know about this. Sometimes, there was a new thought or an incident and her brain filled in the gaps. Occasionally, she spoke to Knight but he repeated what she already knew or, occasionally, less than she knew. A squadron of twenty ships had been put in place high above the North Pole to respond to any emerging concerns.

Disbelieving Knight's claim about Alliance activity, Sally started to look at the nearby stellar systems. She found she could zoom right in to see colonies and people going about their business. It was hard to believe but why wouldn't it be true? It was all so amazing but, then, if she'd travelled back to meet Isaac Newton, wouldn't he have been astounded by her phone? The people in the fort had stared at them as they'd arrived.

She found herself gazing at a star called *EZ Aquarii*. According to the associated bumf, it was just over eleven light years from Sol. As she moved the viewpoint to the sun, she could see three green ships near the star. There was a line at the bottom of the text that suggested atypical solar activity and no further details.

"Does Earth have any ships there and what is the destructive range of a supernova?" Sally asked.

"No," replied Knight, bluntly. "Thirty light years. Why?"

Sally pointed at the screen. When she looked up, it was the first sign of fear she had seen in his eyes. She'd assumed they had everything under control. She was shocked that he was shocked.

Knight immediately turned to the staff and ordered an analysis. Lady Blue popped up from the floor and recognised that *Aquarii* was being accelerated into supernova. That close to Earth, it would wipe out the solar system and the sun with it. It would destabilise this end of the galaxy. This was identified as *mission critical*. A message was prepared for despatch. It wouldn't be sent immediately. This was only a problem, right now. The information would be deposited at the early part of the war. The man they chose for the task looked like a younger version of Knight. Was it the same man, earlier in his life? Maybe it was a clone.

Sally had felt a little buzz of elation that her observation had been validated by another. Was it good that she had helped them? The enemy, the one they'd wanted her to believe was the enemy, were out there. They were green on the screens. The other enemy, the ones who'd stuffed her head full of memories that weren't hers. She felt a bit of a traitor.

Sally noted the reserve squadron had thirteen vessels. She'd looked at them before. An overlapping memory now fading, showed her twenty but the thirteen were as clear as day to her. When had they been called away? Reality challenged her perception. Had the other ships ever been there? As for *EZ Aquarii*, there were no ships at all, green or blue. The system information said there were no matters of interest.

"You are a life out of time," Knight observed. "You see things others can't. The ships were sent over a week ago but you still notice the change."

Still overwhelmed by two memories, without clarity which one was correct, she asked, "Did that mission require all those ships?"

"All seven deployed, but there were a number of other matters that needed attention. Their action represents a change in their behaviour."

This was like playing chess on a computer. When the programme took the upper hand, you could go back a few moves to try again.

"What's the catch?" Sally enquired.

"There's a finite number of available ships to send. You may yet discover the tribulations of trying to arrive at a specific time. Coordinating the separate missions while maintaining the larger defence of the system consumes resources.

"The people we send up and down become weary from the effects of the temporal shifts. Constant exposure to the elements takes an impact on mind and body." In response to Sally's quizzical look, he added, "You must have experienced this yourself? You feel the building is trying to stop you."

Sally raised her head as if to nod in agreement but stopped herself. She felt embarrassed that she'd helped them. She didn't want to be seen to agree with them as well. They'd altered her mind without her permission. It was hard to feel pleased. So, why was there an urge to justify herself? She didn't know how long she would be their guest, an hour, a day, a week and then what? Knight had suggested she should fight but hadn't minded that she'd stayed. If that distant sun had gone bang sooner rather than later, it would have killed her and anyone in the solar system. As she hadn't tracked down Jason yet, there was an argument for maintaining the status quo. It wasn't ideal but it was all she had.

Another memory was trying to catch her attention. It had

flickered at the back of her mind when Knight mentioned resources fading away. It was like trying to sing a song based on half a line of a lyric. She found herself trying to tease out the rest. If there had been a tune, she might have had a chance.

There was a flash of a memory of a large industrial complex. Mechanised lines that started small and ended big: as big as a fighter; as big as a module for a ship. That was the edge of it. She felt the memory was the stepping stone to something greater. When it didn't come, she clung on to this mechanised moment hoping something would trigger later on. No one seemed interested that she was soliciting information from the screen. Numerous facilities and space docks produced vessels. A wing here, an energy unit there, guns here but assembly was done elsewhere. The main construction sites were off world and there were many of them. A single vessel could be built in different locations. There should be a total, somewhere. Production data compared against the ships sent to the front in the last month didn't match up.

Knight spoke to her about the enemy's strategy, which she'd heard but ignored. It was Earth's strategy that drew her attention. Something in one of those memories pulled at her; a puzzle wanting to be solved. It must be big, she reasoned, so where was it?

♟♞♜♜♜♞

Jason was on his way to Earth. His fighter would make it there. So would he, after a fashion. His body might be a block ice by then but he would make it. Some consolation that was.

Fingers and toes were slow to respond and the chill was reaching into his limbs. Jason lost the sensitivity of the stick in his hand. He had to keep looking to see he was holding it. His core remained lukewarm; it was all the suit could do.

He'd done his best to point his fighter where he wanted it to go. The route said Earth was his destination. That was enough. There was little between him and there and all he needed to do was count the minutes to arrival.

A hundred wintry mornings back home were no preparation for this. This calm was the most positive experience he'd had today. If it weren't for the cold and the stress of combat, it would be nice to fly these ships. Fear and cold drained body and mind. Concentration lapsed with each lengthening blink of his eyes.

Numbers on the screen said the rest of the fleet were having a worse time than he. He managed to straighten the forefinger of his left hand and direct it from elbow and shoulder and pushed his arm through what felt like wet cement. His fingertip didn't strike cleanly but it triggered the channels.

Jason's ears were full of noise. In one moment, all the communications channels fired up. Voices clamoured for attention in his headset.

"Fighters have suffered huge losses—"

"They're picking us off at will!"

"We're hanging on."

"Where's your leader?"

"We're thin on the ground here."

"We need a destroyer."

"I can't disengage!"

"I need more ships to crack that shell."

"I'm locked on course. How do I disengage?"

"*India Team*, cover that space."

Jason began to focus on one voice.

"All remaining fighters acknowledge. We're down to roughly three hundred fighters."

Another voice. "That total includes individual fighters damaged and abandoned. There's even a ship way out of position in *Mars Sector H*."

"I see it. Designation *Lima One*. What is your status?"

First there was silence, then Jason's cold-slowed mind realised they were talking to him. Ten thousand ships and someone was talking to him. *L* for *Lima*. *L* for lost, in the middle of nowhere. *Lima One* for the only one left in his team. His helmet display said L1. He hadn't noticed.

"So cold," he said, without realising the words were leaving his mouth. He was not merely cold, he was freezing.

"I see your ship. Ensure the gel is active then aim for *blue dust* on radar. Re-join battle when done."

The gel. Why hadn't he thought of that? It would seal him in. Insulate him. Was it too late though? Did the ship have the power?

"Computer," he requested, his words issuing slowly, "activate the gel."

There was a pause that was long enough to make him wonder if it had worked. Maybe whoever had shared that thought was laughing at him. After a few seconds, a clear and thick fluid poured into the cockpit from behind his back. As it engulfed him, visibility blurred, momentarily. The liquid filled around him. The gel then hardened at the outer edge, and that hardening graduated inwards until an inch from his suit. A moment of fear as he felt trapped within this bubble. Breathing became shallower, faster. Yet, as his arm moved, the harder gel became spongy. He had movement. He felt a little warmth on his neck. Something told him: he was all right here. The gel began to warm up. As the outer surface hardened, it had the effect of trapping most of the heat.

Now, he had to look for 'blue dust' and he turned his attention to the tracker. There was a distortion in his view from the gel; he commanded tracking data be applied to his visor. Tracking pointed out numerous patches of blue dust, among several other colours. The gel, he noticed, absorbed the forces as he manoeuvred his ship.

The blue dust on the radar were fragments, mostly, of debris compatible with his ship, mostly from Earth's own ships. He knew his vessel could self-repair from the first engagement. It was news to him that it could rebuild itself using external material. The outer hull thickening and expanding to fill the gap in the screen. The effect of the gel and the sealing of the crack meant the penetrating cold had been ushered out.

Irregular pieces impacted his hull. When the pieces neither damaged his ship nor bounced off he realised they were being absorbed. The fighter was patching itself up. A dark metal streak spread up the screen. Soon, the new compounds fused with the original structure and, once again, it was a solid ship. Other materials – bomb fragments and other ordnance, spent or unused from destroyed ships, also in the blue – were remade to resupply parts of his ammunition.

Jason's body temperature was almost back to normal when he felt that heaviness that meant a larger ship was arriving. He slowed down but was prepared to move in a hurry, when a single corvette dropped in next to him. He moved alongside and it jumped again.

♟♟♙♙♙♟

"In the weeks leading up to this battle, Earth's forces had developed particular success with a hit-and-run strategy. Reports indicated that the enemy had grown tired of Earth's constant nipping at their heels. The alliance decided to cut the head off the snake with a single, massive assault on the home system. Here, under the watchful sight of her yellow sun, Earth was striking again and again. But, to the dismay of the invaders, Sol's forces were not withdrawing. At least, not far. The Alliance assumed its former member would surrender and promise not to do it again. Instead, they carried on and on. The rates of attrition were the same, but Earth started with less and yet they still they carried on.

Earth's fleet moved like submarines in space. They approached their targets, appeared from amber-space, to gauge distances to target then vanished. Ships winked out from normal space, reappearing unexpectedly and at differing ranges. They appeared near or amongst their foes and disappeared. Some Alliance ships tried to figure out where the Earth ships would reappear next and poured weapon fire into empty space. Others realised, too late, that they had been and gone, leaving behind objects. The resultant explosions left irreparable holes in ships.

In space, even small black shapes stood out amongst the nearby planets and distant stars. In the heat of the moment, they became invisible to the eye. The sensor could only agree with the small signature it detected. Most ships could track a blip on the radar to a zone that eyes said were clear. The bomber got through," Knight presented. His audience was annoyed at the least, uninterested at best. Sally imagined herself in a library trying to find the right book. Occasionally, she found something that looked about right and pressed a button on a screen. Information, that didn't precisely answer her question, would appear. It inspired Knight, as the nauseating library assistant, to add content.

She didn't want to ask him because he might not take it well. They, that is, Knight's organisation, had cheated somehow. They'd found a way to create more ships and crew to put in them. She'd seen, first hand, how they'd gathered the people. The fort experience and the subsequent revealed memories told her. An advanced culture, that is a technologically advanced one she corrected, had hunted their ancestors as if for sport. Definitely not an advanced culture by itself; who would willingly hunt their own? There was something about the factory making the space vehicles that was important. What was it?

♙♟♟♟♟♙

The jump dragged Jason from a weightless state to another via a moment of heaviness. There was no clue in amber space as to how when the ships would exit. He had to be ready all the time. He couldn't lose focus again. He didn't want to be shot at but it beat being cold and alone in the dark of space. His ship's energy level was moving upwards.

There were fighters waiting upon arrival and, reassuringly, they were from his side. They made the numbers back up to nine. Three squads of three. Inside his helmet, the role of *E1, indicating Echo One,* appeared in a corner. He wondered what had befallen team *Lima* but didn't fancy another barrage of video evidence. He hoped they had been renamed, as he had just been, and tried to forget it. This probably meant he wouldn't. It would have been nice to have received some approval, or even a greeting. The faces of *Shark* were on his mind, though he wondered if they were real. So far, they were the only faces he'd seen that looked normal.

This time, the destroyers pushed ahead and pounded the hulls of two enemy ships. Both had the shape of a triangular sandwich, shoved awkwardly into the side of half a baguette. As it passed, there was no light from behind to denote the presence of engines. The squad was told to attack two resupply ships and they had been caught in no man's land, without protection.

Jason's nervous system accelerated up the scale. The gel had retreated and he was now too hot from the stress of it all. *Was anywhere safe?* He had thought the emptiness, between battles was the place to be until weapons fire that had missed its target struck his hull. He had probably been unlucky. Here, in the thick of it, ships fired at each other. If one big ship fired at another and missed, he could be in the firing line.

The small nine flew in behind the big two, then dispersed to attack the nearest ship. Eight went over the top while Jason slid underneath, rotated his fighter, aimed and fired. Energy and kinetic weapons were unleashed at what he called the underside. He knew a long, straight line was unsafe, as it made it easier for the enemy to track him. He bet his survival they would be focused on the bigger vessels. His attitude was punished with a triple burst of red light from a gun at the other side. It didn't so much strike as pound his hull. Even inside his helmet, his ears felt muffled, as the sound reverberated round his cockpit. He felt he'd stood inside a great bell while someone struck it with a hammer.

A voice called to him, asking him to confirm he was okay.

"I guess," he offered. "My ears aren't right."

"It's temporary. It'll fade but it could be one minute or thirty. Meanwhile, next time you're inspired to break formation, notify someone, first. We thought you had a problem."

Jason, suitably admonished, admitted his oversight and was surprised by the next sentence.

"The ship is signalling a surrender. What are your orders?"

My orders? Best to choose something and quick.

"Disable it, then we can move on," he commanded, hoping he sounded more confident than he felt.

"Confirmed. All right team, aim for the energy stores and weapons. Strike with kinetic to break the hull, then energy to bleed the supply."

Shortly after the enemy's power dived into the red, they flew back to the corvette. Jason felt his left ear return to life. It reminded him of his last cold. He had had to angle his head to one side to hear a sound coming from straight ahead. With the helmet on, this wasn't going to work. He wondered if he could change the volume settings to compensate, but he triggered squadron information, instead. It told him they were missing a fighter. He tried to find out which one and spotted it was one of his three. He felt a hole in his heart open up. There was no chatter on the line at all, let alone about that incident. A part of him was grateful but he fretted that they could be talking about him on a private channel.

They moved on to the second ship, which was fighting on against the attack of the destroyers. The other voice sounded on the line again.

"Orders, Chief?"

He felt the pressure in his delay. It was hard enough just to pay attention here but to decide on it. To tell people what to do. They might live or die on his word. *Why me? Who put me in charge?* They'd designated him Echo One. Was that fair on them? Perhaps, they hoped leadership would instil in him some responsibility. Delay would make martyrs of them all. He thought it best to choose now and try to worry about it later. What mattered right now? The destroyers would protect his team. He needed them in one piece.

"Its big guns are a threat to the destroyers but we can fly around them. Focus on them."

CHAPTER 6

I'm not mad, am I? Sally asked herself.

What Sally thought she meant faded away as an image assailed her. She was standing in front of a group of people, addressing them. Some were standing, most were sitting on the floor. Those standing had guns and those sitting did not. Maybe this was not an address, at all. Perhaps an ultimatum. Although it was only an image, someone had declared her as being mad. No, not her. Rather, the person in her position. She felt herself, in the memory, turn to look to the side. There was a mirror on the wall. It wasn't her image in the reflection. There was a woman in her place. The memory faded but she tried to hang on for as long as she could.

Desperate to see the scene once more, she asked herself the question again but there was no repeat of the image.

I'm close, she thought. *The screens are the music and my head has the words. Somehow, I need to combine them to make it fit. Why was 'mad' so important?*

She closed her eyes for a moment to re-see the room. It was longer than it was wide. There were windows down one side. There was the ball again. It hadn't moved since she'd entered the room. It probably hadn't moved in centuries and all the significant events happened around it. No one was near it. No answers came to her from that scene. Was it distracting her? A line to a different tune that interfered with the one she wanted?

Another memory. It was her own. She was sitting on the floor in her bedroom – or, at least, a space made out to be her bedroom.

Why wouldn't it be my bedroom?

She wasn't sitting, she was slumped near the door and her arms hurt. They really hurt. She looked down and could see bruises on them. Some were old, some new, some black and some blue. There was a voice. It sounded familiar.

"Why don't you tell me how you came to be in this building?"

Sally looked up into the face of the speaker. It was the woman from the image with the men and the guns. A little younger here. She was dressed for business.

"Hello, young lady. My name is Victoria. How do you do?"

Sally looked at the woman in awe.

"You can call me Vic. What's your name?"

"I'm Sally."

"Why don't you tell me how you got here?"

Memories of her journey through the many floors of the strange office building flooded her mind.

"It's all been a silly mistake. Jason and I— well, something happened and we were both trying to make it all right again."

Sally carried on pouring out words. Words she shouldn't have shared. Life at home, the boy next door, the other boy down the road. How they came to be here. Her words flowed as water released from a dam.

When Sally had come back to the subject at hand, Victoria slapped her across the face.

"Lies! Which member of the board put you up to this?" Victoria demanded.

"I can prove it," Sally said innocently.

Sally opened her eyes and was back in the room with the screens and new memories. When did that all happen? Sally was sure it was real, but how? It played and replayed. Sally had seen it coming but she had not tried to defend herself. She hadn't raised her arms to defend herself. *Why not?*

The woman from both scenes looked similar, even for the brief glimpse in the reflection. What was that memory about the discussion between Vic and the technician? Some procedure. Why was that suddenly in her head? Where was the link? There was no putting two and two together. She thought she heard Victoria's voice again. She turned slowly to see the same room of people. Men and women were watching blue balls pass by. The angry aunt had gone and Sally appeared to be forgotten in the room. When Lady Blue spoke again, Sally's eyes and ears focused in on her or it. It sounded like Victoria's voice.

Driven by curiosity, Sally moved towards the lady in blue. Nobody moved to stop her. She didn't even think anyone looked up from their tasks. Knight's face was partly turned away but he was smiling about something. She decided to ask straight out but, as she approached, the lady turned to her.

"Your friend. The one who can't tuck in his own shirt. Do you know where he is, right now?"

How— Sally began, in her head.

She wanted to ask so many questions. How did this woman, *Computer*, lady know? Hadn't the lady taken something back from her? Where had all those memories come from?

Is she still in my head? When she'd taken something back, had she really taken something of mine?

She looked up at the glowing woman. Her figure was both static and flowing. Her eyes moved as though she had real pupils. There was something underneath but it wasn't a conventional biological system. There was a sense of foreboding in the eyes that penetrated her own. There was also a murky underlying current in which sharks would have felt at home. Why bother to have thoughts, when the lady in blue seemed capable of pulling them all out?

"Observe."

Lady Blue didn't invite, nor did she direct. It was a tone you may have heard from a seasoned dog-handler. She spoke, not merely with an authority over those around her, but as one that expected only obedience. It presented the epicentre of command, from which ripples of power emanated.

Movement in the blue face stalled, for a moment. It wasn't a long delay but, in the pause for something suitable to view, there was a crack. In time, one might insert the thin end of a wedge, then reach for a hammer.

On the screen in front of them, a large artillery shell appeared, with a purpose as blunt as its shape. Sally had seen it from all those screens. Three wings extended outward through cylinders equal to its length. More of that jumble inside her head, perhaps. It was Earth's main *Fighter*. While it remained static next to them, there was a feeling of movement at considerable pace.

Explosions rocked its movements and Sally's confidence. She had been led to believe Jason was inside, though she couldn't imagine how. It took a moment for the view to retreat to see the flares were manoeuvring thrusters set along the cylinders. Whoever was in there was an adept at the controls. The hull was a dark shade and adorned in an unfamiliar design. It could have been a constellation, if you were being generous.

The focus zoomed out and the little vessel wasn't alone in space. It had eight sisters and they darted from or to something. The point of view continued to withdraw and the nine in a diamond formation were flanked by two larger ships. The view identified them as destroyers, each marked by a number, twelve digits long. Knight mumbled that they had been produced too recently to be named formally. As a unit, they scythed their way through their foes.

One engagement followed another. Sometimes, ships were lost, though they were soon replaced. All were resupplied before the next battle. The more she watched, the more it could be viewed as wolves descending upon stray sheep. The prey was mercilessly torn apart. There was no indication whether a surrender order had been communicated – the attackers ripped through, regardless. Sally requested the columns of numbers to be copied to this new view. The rapid decline of Earth's forces had slowed but the enemy remained ahead on numbers. The home forces had survived the steep learning curve.

Back in the unit, the two larger ships appeared to jump away in different directions. A knowing voice said they had gone to scout different targets for the next attack. Lady Blue pointed to one of the fighters.

"This is the one."

The view zoomed in. The flashes along its surface vanished as it subtly adjusted its direction. The view from the top rotated until the fighter appeared above Sally. The angle then pivoted and it was flying straight towards her. Four circles flew at her, one big one, with three around the outside and stubby wings protruding. The viewpoint lurched and they were in an enlarged image of the cockpit. In front of her, the pilot was oblivious to them. He was smaller than she thought a pilot should be, and covered in a filmy substance. His hands were frantically moving. His right hand was flying the ship. His left was reaching round for something she couldn't see. There was a pause, then his left hand grabbed the base of the helmet at the front. The substance around him drained away into the seat behind him. The screen of the helmet raised, revealing Jason's troubled face.

"What's happening? What's he doing?" Sally asked.

The delay in response made her think her question had fallen on deaf ears. Only after she repeated her question with greater urgency did the blue lady respond.

"He's trying to take back control from me. Unsuccessfully."

Jason gave up whatever needed his unfiltered vision and clicked his helmet back into place. Colours raged on his visor for a moment, then cleared. Sally was still worried, but her logical brain had interceded to generate more important questions.

"What is he even doing, up there? What have *you* done to him?"

"Done? Nothing has been done, as you say, to him. He joined up voluntarily. He is fighting for his planet – unlike, I might add, you."

"You mean you manipulated him?"

"Of course not."

The view changed back to show the squadron around Jason, defending him against an attack.

"You have to let him go!"

"You'll find you can't give me orders, young lady."

Sally's jaw dropped. Infuriated, she tried again.

"Why don't you do something?"

"You don't talk to me like that. No one—"

"Why are you talking? People are being killed!" Sally interrupted Lady Blue with a shriek. The response Sally received was cold and deliberate.

"This is your reward. For all you have done to us. Did you think you would just walk in here and leave? Your overly smart friend with the curly hair, my colleague here pushed him into the smog for his efforts. As for Mr Jason, we have another outcome in mind."

"What is wrong with you?" Sally shouted, desperate.

Painful seconds passed and one, then another of the fighters covering Jason, was put out of action. In Sally's head some of the pieces came together.

Revelations flickered through Sally's mind. The group on the floor without guns, that Victoria directed, were the scientists from the floor above. They were being informed that their work to invent gravity drive had been a great success. But there had been a second, more significant, invention. It was the one that brought this woman to their door. And it was that which had brought one of the scientists to his feet, declaring her mad. *What's her name?* Sally searched the memories. *Yes, I know you now.*

The next scene had Knight presenting to a separate group on the stairs. Then, the shapes in the tanks. Sally called them that because it was better than admitting they were humans. These and more besides, ganged up on her senses. Sally had been manipulated to respond favourably to this woman. In her innocence, she'd disclosed the secrets of the building. In response, they'd pushed Earth into a war. They'd reached into the past and taken boys and girls, grew them in tanks and taught them to fight a war. Meanwhile, these people of the future watched from the side-lines. How could she go home knowing this? History, the future and her present were without hope. So many deaths. So much loss. How many children did those people in the fort lose? Each one of them were now here.

The woman's thoughts swirled in Sally's mind. There was a lot of information. She thought back to her memories of this place. There was little that was positive. She realised what was missing in these extra memories: feelings. There were none. She hadn't the time for friends. Her lifestyle had made what she did next almost inevitable but it came with a single, overpowering emotion. The memory was obscured by the most intense fear Sally had ever felt, the fear of mortal flesh ending. This woman had taken the decision to end her biological life by becoming part of the machine. From that moment, only facts, decisions and actions presided. The machine was a world of ones and zeroes. Cold, lonely thoughts.

Initially, in Sally, there was a searing guilt that she'd shared the building's secret. It tightened her heart and she hid her face in her hands. Yet, if she had been told she could travel to the past or future, she'd have visited for curiosity. *What sort of person kidnaps people, turns them into slaves and makes them fight?* That scientist was right.

Sally felt sick with the discomfort of having a part in it. Inside her, the fear rose until the conversation she imagined in her head couldn't be held back any longer and burst out.

"But it's all so horrible! The pollution. The children taken and brainwashed. I wish none of this existed."

"You don't have that power," Victoria, in a moment of clarity between attacks, declared. "No one does. Only I have the opportunity to undo the past, as I have proven. You are nothing."

Sally smarted and appealed for help. She only found Knight's face, smiling as if this weren't serious.

"Your life is one risk after another. Our present, however, has no risk. It is all planned."

"Survival of the fittest," Sally muttered.

"Oh, my word, no. Survival goes to the richest."

Sally shook her head.

Victoria's eyes glazed over as other matters drew her attention away.

"Lost your heart did you, Victoria?"

"How does someone like you know my name?"

Sally carried on.

"You're not real. Once you stepped into the machine, you gained your immortal soul but lost your mortal one. You can see a hundred lives ending at once. Your computer brain just registers this as ones becoming zeroes. Your heart doesn't spot the loss of life because you don't have one. But then you never had one. An all-powerful Computer. You can do whatever you want – direct the fleet, send people off to die – except, you can't feel anything.

Your existence has no meaning."

Victoria's form flickered then winked out of sight. Sally rounded on Knight, who backed away from her, hands raised and palms facing her.

"Outside of my skill set," he said.

She turned to look at the in-room view of the squadron, fighting desperately. She walked up to it as if she could will Jason's ship free. Inexplicably, the incoming fire stopped and the attackers broke away, the single engines blasting their fuel out the back. The view widened to see the destination: a single ship, all on its own. It looked like a fat, silver pen.

CHAPTER 7

As the destroyer moved back in to finish the job, Jason twisted the stick to evade the larger shots. His fighter jerked around unexpectedly, drawing him away from the heavy exchange of fire. Jason let out a breath he hadn't consciously held in relief.

"My ship is not responding to my controls!" he called in urgently, realising that his lucky manoeuvre could be just as easily a deadly one.

Instructions flooded in.

"I will re-route and come to your aid," offered the captain of the destroyer.

"No, stay on task," ordered Jason, more confidently than he felt. "You need to finish off the enemy ship. The fighters can cover me until my control is restored."

Enemy fighters swept the area with weapon fire and engaged the defensive squadron. Feeling like the chaos was closing in, Jason slammed about every button he could, desperate for something to happen so he could help. He let out a frustrated scream. His ship was not responding.

"Leave me!" he cried. "Save yourselves!"

No one listened, his squadron maintained their positions of cover. Jason resumed his frantic exploration of the controls, shifting the gear stick and slapping the screen.

Suddenly, lights flickered on and the power was restored. Jason didn't know what combination of buttons had achieved this but didn't have time to question it. He made to aim his weapons, when a command came over his headset.

"Quickly! Pull up now!"

Jason looked around, hesitating to follow the order. To his left, a haze of green.

He shouted as he yanked the stick back as hard against as he could, praying for an emergency stop. Momentum carried him forward to enter the field for a brief moment before he reversed out.

His roar extended and escalated into a scream as the energy field was turned on him. Heat burned his muscles in fire and exhaustion. His whole body, from the organs through to the cells, flared. His blood seared through him like lava. His scream changed tone as the magma erupted through his chest to his neck and head. Jason's flight suit dropped its temperature to below zero to counter the heat within. Its impact was limited to the quenching in water of a sword, drawn out from the fire. The surface cooled and hardened, but it would be a long while before it could be touched.

Help me! Someone, help me! Please. I don't want to die. Please. Mum? Help me, Mum. I need you. Make it stop!

His face and back twisted as he tried to brush off a fire that he couldn't stop. His eyelids clamped. He didn't want to see. He didn't want to know. Would he know the difference between too much pain and death? He had to stay awake, to endure, lest it take him.

A repetitive beeping broke through the pain that muffled his senses. He opened an eye to see a small, white light blinking. It was the signal for a wounded man. Tracking told him which way he needed to go. He ignored it. In seconds, he would be bones and dust. The light flashed more rapidly and then switched on autopilot. The computer took control and sent the fighter homeward.

It wasn't fair. I'd just figured out how to fly this damn thing and it kills me, Jason thought, distantly. He didn't even have the energy to be afraid. Everything hurt: his face, eyes, skin, bones and muscles flared in continuous pain. He felt himself separate from his body and, when he couldn't handle the pain anymore, unconsciousness came for him.

♟♟♟♟♟♟

When Sally could take no more, she covered her ears and turned away. She wanted to look back. She couldn't bear to. The blue lady was back and talking to Knight. He came over to talk to her.

"Life is only a three-dimensional concept. It was not designed to travel through time as you have done. The end of the world was coming, one way or another. Instead of fleeing it, we chose to embrace it. Logic says the way out is to find the right move to force a win or a stalemate. However, opportunity takes us in another direction."

Why was he talking to her? How dare he talk to her after this? Sally wrestled back some control of her thoughts. She wondered what his point was. Her head overruled her heart, she voted with her body and turned back to face the screens. After a while, the noise behind her abated. Where was Jason? She glanced up at the panels to see what Earth had left versus what it had lost. There was too much data to see the detail.

♟♟♟♟♟♟

Jason's head swam with strange dreams as his beleaguered body drifted in and out of consciousness. He'd seen what had become of the other squadron. Why was he alive? A ship had turned up to ferry him to safety. The amber swells of that other space between jumps rushed at him in waves then dissipated.

He pictured himself swimming underwater. A lake compressed to the length of a pool, then to barely a metre. With each compression, it became more solid. Instead of the reassuringly clear waters, he saw water with unseen, murky depths. Lurking dangers were crushed into a thin barrier. You couldn't run at it any more than you would expect to survive running at any wall. Condense that vast distance and only the brave dare to step through it to another world. And again. And again. Those who travel far into space, speak of leaving one world and arriving in another. Who speaks of the world in between?

The emptiness of space isn't the same as the bottom of a murky pond. However, unseen dangers waited: dark matter and energies, gravity wells, stars, planets, asteroids and other debris, caught in between.

Sally heard Knight chuntering away behind her. She was unsure if he was trying to instruct or distract her.

"You see, the trim of Earth's largest ships is deceptive. Chameleonic if you will but, rather than just blending in, it hunts too. Persuading the foe that what was real wasn't. It can create a valuable moment of hesitation; it allowed an opportunity to strike first. An image could be presented on the ship's skin of something fleeting, further away, it could look nearer and escaping, or even a vision of the starfield beyond. One moment of doubt to wrestle the advantage in its favour. Fight and flight, while the enemy froze or fled."

Sally watched as Earth's big ships disappeared and reappeared across the battlespace from their hiding places amongst moons and asteroids. A single cruiser flickered across the battlefield. It burst into view in the middle of a squad of enemy vessels. Like a falcon appearing among the pigeons, the group were startled but there was no time to react. No sooner than the aggressor arrived than it was gone. It left behind an expanding ball of energy that melted hulls, cut power and released breathable gases.

Sally worried the Alliance might have powerful weapons too. They might hurt Jason more. She regretted turning away when Jason screamed. Now she didn't know where to find him. Her gaze darted from one screen to another. The approaching tide was gathering power, churning up the beach and pulling away more of the sand that reduced the resistance to the next wave. Earth's latest ships were doing the work of twice their number. But, even to her eyes, they weren't doing enough.

♙♟♙♙♙♙

Knight turned to face Sally.

"The humans here are advanced. Minds can be downloaded into machines while the flesh is repaired. Personalities can move to another place in a different city or planet, as easily as you might move a file. We've moved away from having those little dark spaces out of sight. In your time, with your analogue minds, there are the same old monsters beneath the surface."

"They're there because you put them there," Sally accused him. "Generations of children plucked from their mothers' arms before they can talk. Then grown in tanks and stuffed into cockpits with no more sense of life. The rest of the family grow up in fear as they wonder who will be next. Why have another child, when it could die in front of them? You made the *bogeyman* real. You're not a knight, you're a nightmare."

"You don't understand," he turned away.

Sally realised the enormity of the empire that had been built, up from there. Her challenge that they used slavery to advance their needs was rebuked.

"Slaves make all empires, you know. All the great powers have used them. The strong rule the weak. All the while, the weak call themselves meek. They think they will inherit the Earth. It's not the planet they will inherit, but the soil. All six feet of it will be theirs, while the strong get stronger walking over it. Why would any time have an anti-slavery law?"

"For people like you."

♙♟♚♛♜♝

Jason slumped. His suit worked hard to keep his body in equilibrium. It had heated up to offset a chill, cooled down to counter a fever, absorbed the sweat, filtered and fed back water when he became dehydrated. However, it could offer nothing to save his emotions. As if there was a crack in his own body through which they'd escaped. The extremes began to reduce. He was numbing to the extremes of heat, cold and pain. He was feeling less afraid. He was feeling less of anything. This time he couldn't blame the cold.

He should be terrified. He'd been exposed to the green and he'd seen what became of a whole squadron exposed to its power. He couldn't imagine what he must look like now. Yet, somehow, he was still here. A glimmer of hope reached out to him like a single star in a black night of panic. Perhaps, the images he'd seen weren't real. He looked around as much as his struggling body would let him. His feet rested on the pedals. The controls remained close enough to make him feel somewhat claustrophobic. The suit fitted him. Everything seemed normal.

He *was* alive but his body *was* reacting to the green mist. *What had it done?*

The continuous and frequent rises and falls of energy pushed and pulled at his senses. Tiredness came for him with the oppressiveness of a black hole. It strangled his consciousness and he had little choice but to close his eyes. He'd been half awake when he'd felt his body become heavy as he was drawn into the other space. His eyes had flickered open long enough to recognise the spitting amber. There were about three jumps, collecting casualties. In the transitions between jump and normal space, his body lurched and twisted. As he moved, he could see that the ship had its fair share of dents and damage. He didn't want to know what had happened to them. He didn't want to know what damage he'd taken. He closed off his mind to whatever ordeal his body had endured.

He flicked through the audio channels and picked up details of recent battles and the odd rumour. The fight was not going well for his side. But, the closer the fighting was to Earth, the harder the defenders fought. The Earthers had no ground left to give. In the past their ships had relied on hit and run. Now, where they couldn't run, they were mostly hit. And here he was, suffering from what he didn't know, and people were dying.

The channel changed of its own accord and he was informed that one ship was taking heavy damage. It was one of the largest ships Earth had built: a key target. Jump engines had failed. There was insufficient energy to escape. Fires only burned on decks with air. Numerous enemy vessels had moved in and were pressing for a precious victory.

Jason wanted to be there. Any of the squadrons he'd fought with, especially the last one, could have helped. Instead, he felt empty. He had nothing to offer. He was but one person and one ship and neither were in good shape. His transporting corvette was still on a route home. All he could do was to view the action.

"Show me that ship," Jason managed to croak, and his visor refocused.

It was surrounded by several large vessels and numerous smaller ones, all wanting a piece of the action. A voice came from the dying ship.

"This is the *Oceanus*. A mistiming on our jump drive left us stranded here. We are diverting what little power we have in order to maintain structure. We have energy for one last jump. Do not forget."

Three steady streams of dark green energy struck the ship on her port side. Fighters were engaged in a losing battle in the reducing field between the ship and its attackers.

"*All squadron leaders*, take your teams and go."

The ship was surrounded from all sides. Its dedicated but dwindling supply of fighters continued in their hopeless cause. The ship flickered. On Jason's screen, the enemy, moved in closer. Perhaps, they couldn't bear this magnificent trophy escaping at the last second. They intensified their weapons' fire.

The space where the ship had been, became a large, white sphere. Space reeled against the destruction and, for a second, tore open, unleashing incredible energy that didn't simply destroy but vaporised the ships nearby. It wasn't exactly like looking at the sun, more like watching a cloud passing in front of it. Unstoppable power generated by a fusion core of its jump engines with no destination. A few fighters left the scene at full burn. A couple didn't make it. A voice responded from elsewhere in the fleet.

"*Oceanus*, you will be remembered."

No trace.

No debris.

No dust.

No life.

Another ship, the *Adelaide*, in another battle, was similarly beaten. She'd been struggling for a while in a quiet corner, holding on rather than holding off. Her fighters had long been destroyed. There had been a thought of sending word or warning about the flanking move they had tried to stop. Without a word to anyone, their ship flickered for a moment and it, too, became a large, expanding, destructive ball of energy. The nearby attackers on this occasion had sensed something wrong and tried to escape but there hadn't been time.

♖♞♟♟♟♘

Sally saw the explosions and turned to someone for an explanation. Victoria had her own issues and Knight was hardly likely to speak to her again. A technician spoke in more serious tones.

"In the experimental days of the *drive*, there was a project to compact the *warp tunnel*. The aim was to shorten it so much that ships wouldn't have to move, at all. Sadly, for the crews, forcing two places into the same place created an energy surge that effectively became a feedback loop. The science is somewhat confounding for all but the experts but only one thing can be in one place. Normally, you compress space and move to the next place. But when you condense space so much you don't have to move, your arrival and departure points are the same. Science doesn't like that. You can't be in two places at once. One of the parts has an overload and something has to give. When a ship zero jumps, it includes all the space you've compressed together. The result is energy no longer works in that area. Space isn't made of anything but you can break it."

Sally looked bemused. A minute ago, the Alliance was seconds away from a great success, en-route to its victory. Now, there was a brief pause in the battle. Were they shaken? Earth and its people, it seemed, weren't as weak as they had been led to believe. Small minds in small ships, the Alliance had thought. The original lies spun by the Earthers themselves, who had said size mattered. Who were these people that, with their backs to the wall, would pull the bricks down on top of them, rather than stop?

The sites of the zero jumps caused holes in space and gravity no longer behaved itself. All vessels were told to steer clear.

CHAPTER 8

Jason was determined to remain calm. He felt a rush inside but there was no fear. He fought with the controls, for a moment and let go when they didn't respond. Reinforcements out. Casualties back. When the dented corvette jumped back into normal space, it seemed to be on a path towards Earth.

The temperature fluctuations in his body had eased. The pain lingered in his joints but had lessened. His emotions had faded. He wasn't sure if any of this was good. He'd had an upsetting experience but the upset seemed to have left him.

♙♟♙♙♙♙

Sally had had enough of the screens. What she wanted couldn't be found there. There was no sign of Jason and nothing of the extra ships Earth seemed to have made. Had it been some wild goose chase, set up by Knight, to keep her busy?

The display of the screen flickered on without her supervision. Her attention was drawn to that technician she'd spoken to earlier. He was walking to the edge of the room. As she tracked his movement, a door appeared in the wall, opened and the man left.

A daydream caught her unawares. She was walking down a flight of stairs where, at the bottom, a door opened into a large space. There were no windows and there was a feeling this was all underground. There were hundreds of vertical tubes full of grimy water, each on lines, moving from one end of the cavernous space to another. Self-propelled white cylinders came through a door at the rear. Their ends were sealed. They raised themselves up and into the green tubes. In some tubes they added something and in others, removed it.

She saw other doors. As soon as she looked at one, she stepped through it to another warehouse. This space was at least as large as the last. Multiple production lines created parts, power cells, fighters and modules for the larger ships. Pilots and crews in the room behind and vessels in the one in front. A holistic approach to warfare. Large doors at the end of the construction lines took away the completed parts and people.

Thick smoke, sparks and waste gases were drawn away from the production line by huge fans. Sally's ethereal presence followed them through an exhaust pipe. Different types of waste had specific pipes. At one junction, she followed a blue gas as it wove its way free of the smoke and the heat. After a couple of twists and turns, she found herself travelling towards a bright light. When the end of the pipe was reached, she was floating over a green field. To her right was a forest. To her left, a long hedge. She allowed herself to float up with the gas and turned to look over the area. There were houses on the other side of the hedgerow and, further away, an all-too familiar church on a hill. She blinked and her attention was back in the first warehouse. She returned to the stairs. A few floors up and she recognised the building she was in. *That was it.* That was the answer. The image faded but the memory of it stayed. It was one of those gifts from Victoria, triggered simply by a door. *How many of these were inside her?*

Yet, this was it. She'd searched one place after another to find this build site and they were literally under her nose. In the floors beneath this building, the organisation, headed by Knight and his Queen, had created war machines. To hide their activities, they poisoned the past with the industrial smog. That first floor down with its horrible smoke outside would be culmination of generations of poisoning the air.

Sally felt horrified. She felt that, with Jason, they'd discovered this building. Then, these others had come in and turned this beautiful place into something horrible. Anger welled up inside her. She wanted to shout at them. To tell them how unfair this all was. As that anger threatened to overwhelm her, a single thought dissipated it. She knew that no matter what she said to these people, they wouldn't admit this as a mistake. Their organisation had kidnapped thousands of people from the past and poisoned the rest. This was one deliberate, harmful action after another. They'd given up their humanity in taking everyone else's. *What could anyone say to them?*

She had, through no fault of her own, shared the knowledge of this place to them. If not for her, this destruction would never have happened. It was all on her. *It's not my fault*. She wanted to believe it wasn't. *I've been made to do this*. She knew, she wouldn't be able to get this out from her head. Thoughts like these linger and make you feel like you're the one who's messed up. Sally stood there, wondering which way to turn. Unbeknownst to her, Knight had appeared alongside her. She wondered if he'd seen the weight on her shoulders when he'd spoke.

"It saves on the tears, you know. Our way. There were always tears. When war comes, it is always the civilians who bear the most pain. They wave off their children to fight and, often, die for their flag. Parents who once had simply worried about whether their children would fit in. Would they succeed in their choices and live enjoyable lives? Then, they had to watch as they departed for an unforgiving environment that no one could have foreseen. Instead, we spared the local population that. Then, we took the ones without a future."

Sally turned her back on him. She wasn't listening mostly

because Knight wouldn't. He seemed to revel in all of this; Pleased with his efforts to create chaos out of order. *What can you say to someone who knowingly brought war to peace? What would make any difference?* Perhaps, he was justifying his choices to her. She was grateful, after a fashion, to have her attention drawn to the arrival of new enemy ships. One of them dwarfed all others. The screen identified it as a colony ship. Apparently, it needed to be huge to take all the equipment and personnel to new systems. Considerable energy reserves were required to terraform surfaces and deploy atmospheric units. The top atmospheric layers could be removed from orbit while the lower levels had to be modified by the units. Earth had used it, in the past, to settle its own colonies. It was an expensive process. It had a long, cylindrical body, and a large, spherical head. It was unarmed. What it was doing here was anyone's guess.

Sally couldn't find Jason. They'd come here looking to save Simon but they couldn't save themselves. Her search for Jason's squadrons, *Lima and Echo,* didn't return any data. Vessels had been named and renamed as squadrons were destroyed or adopted. There was no telling what he was called, assuming he was alive. She continued the search, starting with the one-seaters. When that threw up too many results, she looked for people younger than fifteen years old, but there weren't any results.

Knight tried a new angle to focus her attention. He argued against the first level down, she and Jason had experienced, as being her responsibility.

"That floor, the one below your home, isn't inevitable but not our doing. A dedication to years of your throwaway culture is hard to reverse. Eventually, humanity came together as one to overcome it. It is simultaneously your lowest moment and your greatest hope for the future."

What was this idiot talking about? He was trying to gloss over millions of deaths. She felt the fire searing through her veins.

"That pollution. It was added to by you? Did you poison and kill millions of people? Your own people?" Sally asked.

"They're not *my* people. Go back to your Middle Ages and tell me that the black death struck down your people. You don't know them. You don't know their names."

"Yeah, but I didn't send that plague back, to kill them."

"Would it surprise you to learn that, even without our little industrial policy, my past and your future would still be as bleak as you have seen? Our exhaust fumes, down the ages, amount to, at most, one percent of the worldwide pollution."

"Do you expect me to believe that? If you didn't do it, who did?" The fire burned inside her. She would make him realise the error of his ways.

Knight smiled at what he thought was an obviously rhetorical question. When the question continued to hang there, unanswered, his smile returned.

"You don't know?"

Sally shook her head slowly with a glare. Knight pointed at *her*. Sally blinked. Her anger burned on. She started to say something, then stopped. Inside her head was her mother's voice, telling her to think before she spoke. Sally was proving herself right: Knight wasn't listening. It should have calmed her down but, like magma urging to be free, the top blew off the volcano. Her mother could stuff off.

"You are implying this is my fault? I told you about the capabilities of this building. So now your shoulders are sloping and dropping responsibility to me?"

"This is, after all, only one building. Compare that against the vast industrial might of your age."

Sally didn't hesitate. She delivered her final piece, fuelled by anger, with her eyes closed.

"Rubbish! That huge terraformer deploys pods across the surface of a planet to change the gases. You could have done something similar, to fix the problem. You did not. Therefore, I wonder if you did the opposite."

With no response, she opened her eyes but Knight, who had so keenly pointed the finger of blame at her, was nowhere to be seen. Victoria, to whom she had given away so much, became opaque and began to flicker. Sally had to tell Jason all of this, but where was he?

She tapped into systems while the hybrid human-computer was frozen. Messages spooled past. She tried to filter for the unusual. When the system asked for parameters, she stumbled a bit.

"What has happened today that hasn't been seen in the war, so far?"

"Three Earth vessels have self-destructed, rather than retire from combat. Enemy defences have updated flak pattern algorithms. Losses of single crew vessels are higher than anticipated. The resulting tears are causing navigational obstructions. They may affect planetary trajectories. Green fields have caused the death of seventy-four pilots and injured four."

"Yes," she said. "Focus on that. Where are the ships that have been affected by green fields?"

From there, she filtered for returning ships and found several still operating. The early ones had no surviving pilots. Some were further out in the solar system. Only one was coming back to Earth. It was coming here. Almost right outside.

It must be him, she hoped.

As the fighter returned, Sally ran to the end of the room where she'd entered. There were a few, tentative seconds wondering if she would be allowed out. She closed her eyes and walked forward, with her hands outstretched. She opened her eyes to find herself in the all-too-familiar white corridor. She ran to the main door, which opened before she reached it.

At the top of the path down, six fighters were parked below. Two were battered and broken. One appeared to have a pilot, still wearing his helmet. If the other had a pilot, he or she had been lost in the explosion that had ripped open the front of the fighter. Their self-repair mechanisms were working, after a fashion. The one that had its cockpit torn out would need extra help. She didn't want to think of what had become of its pilot. But, a dangerous thought added, *what if it had been Jason*? Yes, he'd been alive when she seen him last. His ship had appeared to have been in one piece but this was a war. It could have happened to him. No. she couldn't picture it. She didn't want to imagine it. She tried to deny her increasing fearful thoughts of it by sprinting down to the fighters. If she could reduce the time between now and confirming what was true, her thoughts wouldn't have the time to create such a horror. A tear escaped an eye in the cool outdoor air as she ran.

The one with the pilot had patchwork repairs. Vapour streamed from both ships. She didn't dare touch either, in case they were too cold from space or too hot from re-entry. Either extreme could take the skin from her fingers and also use her to patch themselves up.

When the canopy of the other finally opened, the pilot eased himself up. He climbed out and lowered himself to the ground one careful step at a time. He went down on one knee and looked to be praying to whatever gods he followed, perhaps for gratitude at his return. When he stood up, he was as tall as her father. His attention was on his hands – or the suit around his hands. He ran his fingers along his arms and body.

Sally looked up to see a couple of fighters above. Maybe Jason was in one of those. The screen implied he would return to from where he had left.

The man tried to take off his helmet but instead, raised the visor and looked at himself in the glass of the canopy. The two ships descended through the clouded sky. Each one elevated Sally's spirits until they, too, revealed no one inside.

She was confused. She swivelled on the spot to see if other ships were coming from a different direction, but none came. She was conflicted about heading back to the building to figure out what was going on. Were Knight and Victoria – *the Queen*, Sally thought – amused? She heard the man move towards her.

She wondered if Jason was so badly injured that he had been taken somewhere else. Was he even alive? She berated herself for 'doing a Jason' and rushing out of the door before being certain he was coming here. If she'd stayed inside a little longer, she could have found out for sure where he was headed. It was foolish of her to think he had returned here. *Useless*. She could hear her mum, berating her.

He could have been redirected somewhere else, perhaps to a medical unit. But that wasn't right. The man in the recently returned ship had landed here and no one was taking care of him. Dead or alive, you'd think someone would at least come out and check. If there were any medical facilities, they weren't at the top of the priority list.

"Hello?" said the man.

Though she was anxious, she responded.

"Hi. Are you all right?"

It was a polite but bland thing to say to someone who had been through who knew what. She found it difficult to look at the stranger, while wanting to scan the clouds. There was no response from him; he simply regarded her. He was calm, despite whatever he had been through. More small talk bubbled through her head and out of her mouth.

"What squadron are you in?"

He gazed at her for a moment then looked up. His eyes looked friendly. She glanced at his helmet.

"Are you going back up soon? You know, in a new ship?"

His eyes became quizzical, then he had another attempt at removing his helmet. This time his thumbs reached some key point inside. There was a barely audible click that widened the base enough for it to be lifted off his head. While she waited for his transformation from a pilot to a human, she cast her eyes back up to the clouds.

He stroked his neck. Maybe he had had a problem with his voice and couldn't speak straight away. He reminded her of an old friend. He had a pleasant face, but was there confusion in it? He didn't look injured. Well, nothing obvious. And he seemed to be able to move around all right.

"Sally?" he asked, seeming surprised at his own voice.

How did he know her name?

"Do I look so different?"

Oh no! No. No! This can't be right. It can't be. Can it? Sally thought, her head spinning.

The puzzlement on his face mirrored her own. This was a joke and a bad one, at that. Jason must, even now, be flying around.

Maybe he sent his commander or someone down to talk to her, first? What fact would only Jason know? A secret password.

Her mind was rattled but she poked around inside for a something out of the ordinary. When she found it, she knew it was the right question.

"What's the name of my younger sister?"

Hesitation. *Was it doubt?* She wanted him to answer but also not to answer. She wanted him to be alive but not this. This wasn't fair. Fighters were coming and going now but none were landing here. The sky high above was a staging area, a holding pattern for arrivals and departures. None of that mattered, anymore. All the ships in the world could land here.

"Do you mean Caitlin or Abigail? If it was Abigail, I asked her the way to the shop, but she wouldn't talk to me until you had."

There it was. The truth. The hard, bitter truth. She dropped to the floor, her shoulders defeated and shaking. She had been building up a world of blame to hurl at him. *All your fault. Rushing off again.* But he didn't need that now. She didn't need it to say it. She needed something. She spoke in a voice between tears and despair.

"What happened, out there?"

He stumbled through an answer. The energy field had briefly touched him. A little had been too much. He'd seen it affect others. A squadron of older men had flown into it. They'd been in it longer than him and had been aged so fast. They'd died of old age in their seats within a minute. Jason had been in the energy for a few seconds but the experience had left its mark. Silence brokered a discussion between two trapped parties.

"What the hell are we going to do now?" demanded Sally.

He stood there for a while, looking around, wondering what to do and even what to think.

"I want to go home but I know I can't. Not exactly."

"We'll never be together. We won't even be friends. What kind of future are we going to have? No one will ever believe this."

♟♙♕♙♙♙♟

Jason simply stood there. A stranger in his own body. A part of him wanted to cry but the rest of him didn't understand why. He wanted to comfort Sally and he wanted to hold her. He wanted to say his body felt wrong but he had no feelings on the matter. Not sad, not happy, not angry, not anxious. He just was.

Sally looked back at the building up on the hill. In the floors below, there were people being grown in tanks. *Could she be added to it?*

No, that wouldn't work, she thought. *Even that process takes months.*

They could go back in time, modify the programming, somehow. The building's custodians showed no indication they would help her. They took what they wanted, used it and threw it away. None of it would work. No amount of going back or forward would solve this problem. Her friend had grown up without her. She'd wanted them to grow together. She wasn't sure how he'd felt about her. If he was interested, she was sure there could be something between them. Now, there was nothing. They'd come here to save Simon, somehow. And what had they achieved? Simon was on life support; Jason was right, he couldn't go home. What had that left her with? Nothing. Inside, she gave up.

Silence reigned. She tried to fight against the tide of emptiness and stand up straight. She transferred her weight from left to right and back again. She couldn't look at Jason but knew she needed to. She would want him to look at her.

She'd been chased, shot at, drugged, experienced memories that weren't hers and been beaten black and blue. Some memories were hers, but she didn't want them any more than the others. She had been attacked by a dinosaur, seen the end of the world and been terrified by it. She'd seen the near future and been confused by it. She'd seen the bits in between and hadn't much liked them, either. And for what? For him to be taken away while his facsimile was standing right in front of her at the same time. There had been the briefest suggestion of more. It had been uncovered just before all this started. Jason's reaction had been, well, very Jason. And here they were. Jason had paid the price for his actions.

Reluctantly, but inevitably, she approached and hugged that which had once been the boy she been drawn to. She felt his arms around her and needed this to be forever. For a moment, she was him and wanted to be him. They had to go now, quickly, before she had time to change her mind.

"Take me there." There was an urgency in her voice.

"Where? Back to the building?" said Jason, somewhat puzzled.

"No, to the place where you changed."

"Why?"

"There's nothing left here."

"What do you mean, nothing?" he challenged.

"For us." She'd wanted to say, *for me*. Why wasn't he being Jason? Why wasn't he rushing now, of all times?

"There will be others. People move on when the circumstances aren't right."

"Why are we here, Jason? Not just standing here. We came here to help Simon. Remember? Why did he even come into this building in the first place?"

Jason glanced at the building. If there was an emotion on his face, Sally didn't see it. He didn't respond to her challenge in the way she expected. He'd changed inside and out. What had become of the boy who'd run off before his brain could catch up? When he'd been punished in the past, he'd told her of being grounded: more homework, less phone time. Except, his dad relented sooner. Perhaps having an undistracted son was more of a distraction to him. The modern phone could be a replacement for the thumb to suck on in times of distress. Without his mother, perhaps his father had no one else to share the burden of the upbringing of his son. At home, Sally had been made to feel she was a burden. There was little there for her to return to. What could she do now? The friends her parents wanted her to see weren't as interesting as her neighbours. Whichever way she looked, the immediate future was bleak.

Simon had lost his future. Sally's father had spoken with the doctors who'd said the diagnosis wasn't good. Weeks, maybe. Months, unlikely. And she and Jason were the weaker for it. What future was there for Jason? Where could he go? He couldn't go home, not with her. He'd lost his present with her. How long would she have to wait, to grow up, before this man in front of her, who was, even a few hours ago, her best friend? Time can pass slower for those with the longest to wait. Without Simon or Jason, where did that leave her? There was Caitlin, of course, and a possibility of Abi. Was that part of a future without Sally? Did her parents plan for three or was it always two? If she went back, would Sally's law still apply or would it be Simon's?

The torn apart fighter was reason enough not to go. In a world full of possibilities, Sally felt she had few that were hers to own. If they didn't work out, then what? Here now, there was something.

Jason offered no reply, only an upwards look. Sally's eyes followed, briefly. Beyond the clouds was an unfolding horror. Death was being handed out and for what? She'd be lucky to get where he'd been hurt.

Sally was frustrated. Simon was no better off, Jason would never be the same and she had nothing to live for. What mattered to her, what mattered most was the three of them. They were her world.

Jason was clearly trying to protect her when he pointed out another issue.

"The green energy is quite a distance away. We'd have to hitch a ride with a larger ship and they may not do it because we asked. The other point worth mentioning is this other fighter here." Jason pointed to the one torn apart. "This outcome is a very real possibility. What do you think of that?"

Sally didn't respond to that. Looking at the broken vessel a final time, she noted the seat inside was unscathed. It was possible the pilot had survived and was somewhere being tended or mended. The pilot may have had a chance. The time to act is now.

"Are *you* sure?" Jason queried.

"Of course. Of course, I am. Let's do this, while there's still time."

"My fighter can fly but I'd rather not take it, especially when there are others. You jump in the one on the end and I'll take the one next to it."

"I don't know how to fly," she protested.

"Neither did I, until I sat inside. It kind of teaches you as you go."

"Could we take a two-seater?"

"I don't think there are any. And now I've changed, there is no space for both of us in one. Besides, if we go together, we will both age. I don't want to see what happens if I go through it twice."

He touched the front of the canopy and fished out the helmet and suit.

"Put these on while I give you an overview of the controls."

Her eyes were wandering and he realised she hadn't paid one iota of attention to him or the displays. She appeared to be looking between the canopy and the floor.

"There's not much space when you look at it from here but it is comfortable. That field must consume a lot of energy, so they won't be able to keep it up, for long. Look here."

Sally's eyes followed his finger but her ears were still hearing his scream. That scream. It went on far too long and, as it changed in tone, he must have aged with it.

Jason pressed a few buttons to start the ship's pre-flight process. She sat in the chair, felt the straps press on her shoulders then the helmet was pushed down onto her head. Without another word, he tugged on the top of the canopy to pull it shut.

"I'll be nearby. If you need to ask a question, speak and I'll be there."

As the canopy shut, she heard it lock. She moaned quietly and pulled against her straps, pushed against the canopy. It was no use. She was trapped. Pressed in against the seat and bottled up in this box. She wanted a magic pill solution. Not to be stuck in a small box. Her heart pounded against the inside of her chest like, it too, wanted to be out. She fought against rising chills of her terror in an attempt to make herself equal to Jason but it only made her worse. She would have to be strong. Somehow. Into her ears came his voice.

"The computer should refresh you on the basics of flying. That'll take no more than a minute, by which time the ship will be good to go."

Sweat rose from her. The helmet didn't feel right. Her hair stuck to her head and felt out of position. The volume in her ears was too loud but she was too afraid to say. There was still time. Time to stay here on the ground. Not to fly in this windowed coffin into a true horror. Debris and flak and ships and explosions would each tear a hole in her ship and suit. All had the power to suck the life out from her little vessel, leaving her with nothing. She would become one more statistic in a battle so large only a screen could see it from end to end. She wondered what would happen to her if Jason was killed. That made her feel so cold.

The ship hummed, then, with a small lurch, the view angled up and the ground fell away. Jason's fighter was close. The display was small but full of colour. One of the dials flickered red and she squealed. Jason's calm voice asked her which one was malfunctioning. It took her a few seconds to say how many down and across it was.

"That's the undercarriage. Press it, quickly."

She did and it stopped flashing red and became green.

"Some systems are automatic. That one shouldn't have needed you to act on it. The system must be busy," Jason told her.

♟♙♙♙♙♙

Jason felt his body press into the seat as he took off and accelerated upwards for the second time. It didn't feel right but nothing did. War was all it was cracked up to be. He was in tears when he left before and in terror when he saw *Shark* team. Those pictures were still unnecessary, though now they were in his memory, serving as a warning. People go off to war. Mostly, they come back. Mostly. He'd come back with his fighter – or what was left of it – but he had changed.

As he powered upwards, he scanned his systems and sought out Sally's fighter as it wasn't immediately behind. There was nothing else taking off around them. He adjusted his trajectory to intercept it. As the clouds moved away below him, he glanced up at the mirrors and saw the shrinking fields and towns. Somewhere below was the building into which Simon had gone. It was all the same colour down there now and he pondered if all the buildings were the same colour on top as at the ground. He decided to mark this location on his tracker in case he couldn't find it on the return. While it was on his mind, he had better mark Sally's fighter.

Why am I doing this? Didn't I learn the last time?

Lima Nine was a memory and so, he reckoned, was all of *Lima* squad. And probably *Echo* team, too.

♙♙♙♙♙♙

The building around which so much of their recent lives had centred shrank and faded into the landscape. There were cities, down there. On any other day, they would have taken Sally's breath away, with their exquisite designs and jaw-dropping towers. She would have loved to have walked around them with Jason. Instead, the ship swept through the clouds, drawing a brief, spiralling trail. As the clouds faded from view, the blue above her slipped away as the painter added extra black to the image. When there was no more blue on the palette, gold and silver were mixed in, to form the stars. The sight was followed by a brief crackle along the edge of the canopy as the pressure shifted to zero outside and the temperature dropped far below that. The fighter's power core generated some gravity but it wasn't the same as being on solid ground. The pull on her was back into the seat rather than from underneath. There was a sense of looking up from a chair that had tipped over when you'd leaned back too far. Her hand fumbled the stick and her fighter drew away from Jason.

"What are you doing? Pull back in behind me, to be my wingman."

She didn't know what a wingman was. She felt a pinching at the back of her head. As she leant away from the seat, a thought came to her that said, a wingman followed the leader in formation. She looked at the controls and didn't know how to make it a reality.

"Computer. Follow that fighter. Be the wingman," she whispered, hoping it would hear her but Jason wouldn't.

The autopilot took over and tucked in behind Jason's ship, about a mile behind. It dipped left and right just enough to be nauseating. When Jason asked her to close in, she directed the computer accordingly. Closer, as an instruction, wasn't good enough. She had to mark the distance in time or distance. It was another metal box that needed specific instructions. Other fighters gathered around them as the *Poseidon*, once again, returned to Earth's orbit. Numerous fighters, burnt, blackened and some simply torn apart, spilled out from the returning ship. These were just the ones that had something to salvage. They were left to drift. Repair bots were deployed from the large space dock structure to collect anything worthy of salvage.

The *Poseidon* was still going but had seen a bit of action. One corner was missing, leaving a few bent and twisted struts extended from the absent point. Even from here, Sally could see flashes of light from the fighting. Her display indicated there was no single battle. Every ship was its own front line. Tactics and strategy had brought the war here. Technology and guile were keeping the enemy at bay.

The automated systems in Sally's cockpit oscillated in response to the discharge of sweat from her body. It cooled her, recycled the sweat into water and hydrated her. The water fed into her mouth and, when it was unwelcome, it spilled inside her helmet.

She tried to free herself of her helmet. With both hands firmly pressed to the underside, next to her ears, she pushed. She twisted her head, bent over as far as she dared without touching the virtual console. There was no movement here, either. She would have as much chance of removing her own head. She directed the computer to remove the helmet but there came no reply. She glared out through the window, as if to say this was all the fault of the stars.

CHAPTER 9

The *Poseidon* dropped them in a different quadrant of the solar system, then jumped away. Almost instantly, the tracker identified a squadron of about twelve enemy corvettes on an intercept course. Was it paranoid of Jason to think they had come for him? It was optimistic for the *Poseidon* to think he could handle them alone. Even one enemy vessel would make short work of two little fighters. It would take the enemy about thirty seconds to hit firing range and the fighter couldn't generate enough pace to evade them. Jason accelerated to full speed and confirmed Sally was right behind to at least try to escape when that heavy sensation returned.

An Earth vessel arrived. What was left of it blocked his view of the attacking force. It was a miracle it had managed to get here. Matter and flames spilled from it. An information strip informed him the ship was called the *Gabon*. Of the hull there was little to report beyond the skeletal structure, just exposed machinery, torn panels and broken struts. There was a hole wide enough to drive a lorry through. Nothing identifiable, human or machine, had survived the damage. The glow from the engines intensified. Half a dozen fighters spilled out around it, then all turned and headed towards Jason. As they approached, he received a message to continue at full burn.

He rotated as advised and, checking Sally was with them, all eight headed away. He reserved a display in his visor to view the unfolding scene, behind. He did not imagine the battered ship would hold them off for long.

The corvettes slowed down to align themselves into two uneven formations. One would finish off the *Gabon* while the other took a wider route to pursue the evading fighters. Jason was sure the glow from the *Gabon* was much brighter now. The ship appeared to flicker. Stars beyond the ship blurred, twitched then stretched as it fired up its jump drive. Dark energies poured out from the sides. As soon as the corvettes began firing at her, the dark snapped back into the ship. For a moment it shrank, then was suddenly replaced by a vast silver ball of energy. It consumed all but the fighters. Jason couldn't push his stick away from him any further but that didn't stop him trying. His fighter shuddered at the speed it was going. All power on his vessel went dead from the blast wave. The eight fighters drifted out of formation. No debris escaped that flare. A superheated ball of plasma rose and fell from the destroyer.

Jason couldn't even check his power supplies. There was no power coming through to the cockpit. The buzzing behind him stopped and his visor display turned on, slowly. A few red, glowing embers in the engine intensified. He waited as the lights changed from red to green via amber. When most sensors had turned green, he put a finger on the holographic keys and checked his ship and Sally's. Thrust looked a bit intermittent but he reckoned he could call upon eighty percent power. It wasn't clear whether the engines had been damaged in any way or if there was just a power drain. Communications went amber on his panel and there was a good chance the same systems would work on hers.

"Sally, are you okay?"

He thought she said yes. He could see her waving at him. Jason checked on his new squadron and they brought him up to date on the situation. The channel crackled with interference. He brought up a map of the solar system. Most parts had clear signals. Some faded out, wobbled or failed to materialise. One such unidentified piece in this puzzle was not far from their locale. It must be where the *Gabon* made its sacrifice. There were now nine such zones on the map and he marked them with one finger while highlighting all as a navigation threat.

He tapped a forefinger against the helmet in front of his lips and considered where the green zone was. He wouldn't have wished for Sally to miss out on ten years of her life but she had been sure this was what she'd wanted. He remained numb. How long would his body take to come to terms with the change?

Did the green field ship still exist? Would it have become a victim of the battle by now? Neither side was going to be bothered by eight fighters. He had time to check it out. He tapped in a few parameters and waited. Maybe the aliens could reverse the process, make him young again.

Yes, that could work, he mused.

He tapped on his helmet, trying to ignore the second thought at the back of his mind. What would be the benefit for them? Here they had come, light years from home, in the death throes of a war which had taken many souls. Why would they switch their rays into reverse to help out the enemy?

The search revealed a potential green field target and the system reckoned it was an hour and forty minutes away. That could be a long journey. He informed the squad this was a target, without stating the intent, and requested solutions. A communication was issued by a member of the squad on a different line. Two minutes later, a corvette, insignia of *Lafayette*, appeared next to them. It confirmed it would deliver them to their destination on the proviso they followed it to its next assigned priority. That sounded fair, assuming they survived.

Jason started to feel heavy again. He warned Sally they were about to jump. He could make out a wave from her. He thought he could see her hand on the window. But it stayed there, for longer than you would have expected for a wave. It made him wonder if all was really well, over there. Perhaps she didn't want this. He couldn't blame her. He didn't want this but he knew of no way to undo it. The weight slipped away and he felt light again as they returned to normal space. The *Lafayette* reported problems with its engine since its last engagement. They would work on it and give them an update, shortly. Meanwhile, the squad was to hold tight and use trackers and eyes to scan the area.

A communiqué came through from Sally, followed by a plea for a personal exchange between his ship and hers. No eavesdroppers. He waved his fingers through a series of coloured lights and a secure line was set up. After he said hello, it was quiet for a while. He thought he could hear words and spent some time trying to clear up the signal. He was toying with the volume at the lower end of the scale when she shouted out words so quickly he couldn't make them out. Initially, he thought there was a problem with the line. There was some noise and it took a few buttons to make it clearer but her words came through too loud.

"I am in a flying coffin waiting for an appointment with someone who is a better shot. There has to be a better way than this? What if we find this thing and it sends me off to an extreme? I could end up as an old woman. Then what?"

The signal went dead. The sudden quiet on the line was as pleasing as the shouting had been shocking. In the pause, he received an unwelcome epiphany. He'd been stuffed into this suit. It had been too big for him, then but it fit him now.

They knew! Jason thought. *They sent me out here. They knew.*

He should have been angry. Instead, he simply registered surprise at the thought. The surface of his skin tingled in the way it had done on the very first step down to find Simon.

The corvette reported its engines were operational again and they were ready to jump. He felt the pressure as the ship moved into amber space. He thought of the last time he'd seen Simon on his feet. His heart no longer registered the loss. All that remained was the inescapable number. One minus one equalled zero.

When they returned to normal space, he noticed a light. It flashed slowly at first, then picked up. It took him a minute to notice something new on the comms panel. Why was it doing that? He reached out for it and touched it but it flashed on, regardless. Was he in a dream, where something looked familiar but nothing made sense? He shook his head and leaned forward and realised the channel was still locked down. He wafted his hand on a separate combination and the flashing amber became green. Then he heard the signal that had been trying to come through.

"Are you all right, Squad Leader? Repeating, this is the *Corvette Lafayette*. We have made the jump as requested. Your target is three minutes from this location. We would have arrived closer but there is a lot of debris. The vector has been linked to your track. Confirm your status. Are you all right, Squad Leader?"

"All good," he replied, as the objective swam into focus.

More debris buzzed around him. In amongst it, the vessel he had been searching for was unprotected. It was possibly using the track of clutter as a shield until more ships became available. He called on Sally.

"The target we have been looking for is only a few minutes away. If you want to pull out now is the right time to say."

Nothing for a few seconds, then a simple green light on the communications panel. It was as good as a 'ready when you are'.

Jason pushed his stick forward and the squad fell in line. They weaved through pieces of scrap. Some, he reasoned, would be too small to see. One piece was larger than the corvette that delivered them here. He called to the ship to advise caution and keep clear.

Jason didn't need to see that sequence again of the effects of the green. He remembered it too clearly. Men became old, became dead in seconds. Lines appeared next to their eyes. Before the teeth were blocked from sight, they turned yellow. Hair turned grey, then white. Lenses clouded over. Eyes looked wild and fearful. When there was no more ageing left, the screams stopped and the eyes stared on into the eternal distance. Somewhere in the all-encompassing night sky, their little ships, otherwise undamaged, disappeared into the deep. Others would be corralled into orbits around the bodies circling Sol. Each one a grave.

He thought of his own brush with fate. In the space of a minute, he'd become a man. By rights, he should have had a beard down to his stomach. How much had the helmet and suit worked to keep it to just stubble? Still, there was a sandpapery feel to his neck. In the quiet phases, he couldn't help but check himself over, still not quite believing it had happened.

They caught up with the target soon enough. A disappointing mix of brown spots on a tired white background marked it out. It barely moved. It was either dead and floating or low on power. The green was hazy but it was definitely there. Sally barely brushed it, first time out. And the next three times, too. Brushed was being generous. Missed was more accurate. Jason could see she wasn't committed to it, not that he blamed her. It had been a decision in the heat of the moment. There had been plenty of thinking time between then and now. Was this worth the risk of losing her completely? He decided to relieve her of the pain.

"The *Lafayette* is keen to move on to the next mission. One last pass and we'll call it a day."

This time, she flew right at it. He told her to pull up but she pressed on. He heard her frantic breathing over the channel, followed by shouting.

"Nothing's happening. What am I doing wrong?"

Half a scream, half a sob came through, loud and clear. He

drew his fighter up alongside. In spite of her release from this destiny, he could see her hands pressed against the unforgiving canopy.

"I can't do this. How can I make it stop? Help me. Someone. Please I can't take any more of this. Please."

Maybe the target was out of power. Jason felt cheated. Given how little he had been exposed to the green mist, it should have left her looking like a pensioner. Instead, she was fine. Well, she was still the Sally he knew. She sounded some way from fine.

The other pilots drew up behind him. If they were puzzled by Sally's behaviour, they didn't say. Jason recognised the threat of the ship and requested a sustained burst of fire. They would fire from this range for safety. Their on-board targeting systems lined up and delivered the assault over the short period. As they turned, analysis indicated over eighty-five percent of their shots struck the hull. Whether it did any serious damage, he might never know. It was the best he could offer. He informed them they were done here. They weaved a path back through the debris, passing through any blue dust offered. Jason kept an eye on the mirror as they made their way back to the destroyer. He was satisfied this new group of fighters were determined to stay with him.

As each new present ticked into the past, another drop of hope of this being a bad dream faded. In those dull spaces between the bursts of intensity, he realised he couldn't go home. The person outside was a man but inside, who was he. Was he a boy? No, not even a teenager. His insides had aged at least as much as the surface. He had a dad who wasn't much older than he now looked. What would he tell him that would make any sense? No one would recognise him. He could go anywhere in time except home.

There was neither excitement nor tension in his actions. He moved the stick forward a touch to increase the speed and risk.

It should have increased the excitement but there was nothing. When one of the fighters said they couldn't keep up, he slowed down. As they had stuck with him, he felt honour-bound to stay with them. He found solace in focusing on others. The wreckage thinned and the emptiness of space returned. Still moving forward, he rotated his craft around twice. He was a long way from home, however he looked at it.

On the small tracking screen on his visor, he identified the slightly weaving shape of Sally's fighter, behind. They had found the green fog but, on Sally, there had been no effect. In truth, he was grateful. He wouldn't wish his own experience on anyone. Let her grow old in her own time.

The fighters grouped around the *Lafayette's* sides and waited for it to jump them to their next target. News came in that alien home systems were under attack by Earth ships. Jason thought there was a muffled cheer on the line to support this. Why weren't those ships here, helping with the defence? Would some of the attackers would be forced to breakaway?

The weight returned and there were three jumps. The first couple lasted only a few seconds. When they were released from the second, tracking picked up a ship, dead ahead. Possibly a five-minute sprint to engage and he was surprised when they jumped again. This last one was barely enough to fire up the ship's engines. They were out as soon as they went in. They returned to normal space so close to the enemy, he had to fire, immediately.

♙♟♚♛♝♞

Sally's initial panic had subsided. Her spirit had railed against being trapped in this tight space. She reckoned this could be endured by others, she would learn to manage it too. It took her a while to realise the other fighters had people in them and they could cope.

She recognised the need to be small and manoeuvrable, as it was harder to hit. But, when you were hit, it probably wouldn't take much to damage or destroy you. Then came the other thought, which wouldn't let her rest and it reminded her that it wasn't small in here, it was compact. On and on, the thoughts battled each other for dominance. When the ship felt small, light and stable, she tried the controls a little and found them making more sense. When she felt the closeness of the canopy, her movements became erratic and the computer regained control to keep her in formation.

The overriding thought, the one that beat back the others, was that the green mist had had no effect. She wanted to be with him, that was true. But she didn't want to be changed, not really. What if it had made her old? It could leave her in her thirties. Would he have to go back in the field, to catch up with her?

What am I going to do without him?

He seemed to be taking it well. Maybe it hadn't really hit him.

God knows what he is going through and he was so calm about it. If he can, then I can, too.

She knew in her heart it was going to be difficult but she could be there for him. She'd been pleased, in a coherent moment, to have figured out how to locate and track another fighter. So, she had locked on to him. This made his ship glow red in the hologram-radar on her visor. Was her engine overheating? The back of her head felt warm.

The jumping thing was just bizarre. The closest she could relate it to was the school bus going over a humpback bridge. Week after week, the same journey in the same coach went over that bridge. That rising and sinking feeling never faded. She told herself it wasn't exactly like that, of course, that would be stupid. They sank from the heavy, amber humpbacked bridge into the lighter emptiness of beyond.

After the third, the red fighter began firing at a green bowtie, the size of their school gym. It was more generous than saying it was two large triangles that had been shoved together. She began firing, too. Just hitting it was challenge enough and she was happy with that, for a bit. Happy until a voice came through her speakers, telling her to focus on its weapons. It wasn't immediately clear how to do that, so she fired in the direction the others were shooting. More ideas came to her and she knew a way to isolate specific parts of ships.

Driving this stupid thing was an obstacle in its own right. It was fighting her. It wouldn't let her sit still either. How can you shoot at something when you're moving about all over the place? Once Jason and the others had blown up a number of the weapons, the big ship had moved in. It fired a couple of large, white balls at it that hit the surface like ice cream, melting really fast. But, as the ice cream melted, so did the hull. The first one burned a shallow, if wide, hole at the centre of the bowtie. The second went straight through but it didn't reappear on the other side. Bowtie died in that moment. All its lights went out and it stopped firing back.

She moved her ship in behind Jason again. She'd activated a semi-automatic pilot but something wasn't right. There should have been eight of them but she could only count five.

That was sad. I wonder if it was because I wasn't shooting at the weapons, as the others were.

She could be next if she didn't pay attention. The nerves returned.

The controls kept being taken away from her but she was still in one piece. She knew, somehow, that the computer recognised where she wanted to go and put her there. That didn't make sense to her, so she tried talking out loud rather than in her head. The more she talked, the more sense it all made.

Where a pilot flew from A to B, the computer-assisted navigation made it happen. The issue with combat is the opposition's frustrating incessancy to shoot back. This made it hard to stay focused on a target. Energy weapons, flak and fragments hurtled towards and exploded near you. The human brain may not be able to react in time or prioritise the greatest threats. A human can't see three quarters of the threats, not at the speeds the objects are travelling. Therefore, it was determined that a human shouldn't have to. While the pilot is flying, the computer will identify, track and prioritise each threat. It moves the ship left, right, up, down or alters the speed to weave a path through the danger. While you want to fly in a straight line, there may be a few deviations, small or noticeable, on the way. Some threats were unavoidable, no matter how much intervention there was.

CHAPTER 10

They didn't travel to the next fight in *humpback* mode. The engagement came to them. Space was a big hole with nothing to hide behind. It came as surprise to be fired at. When the action was underway, Sally was midway between the four remaining fighters. Red was flying behind the lead fighter. It was so weird. She could only see him because the scope said he was there. She had turned it off, for a few seconds and could only see space, the sun and little in between. The fighters were small and fast; it was hard to pick them out even knowing they were there. It made her feel so cold to think you could be flying alone and never know it. She flew at a tangent to the others while her attention strayed.

A burst of plasma fire scattered through the space in which their squad was passing. White balls of light trailed from right to left. One them clipped the red fighter in front. She held her breath as Jason span anticlockwise, temporarily out of control. The rotations eased and he drew back into the formation they were in. She was so proud that Jason was equal to it all. Another burst of plasma forced her to push down on her stick, to avoid it. Jason was slower to respond, this time. His ship was hit, full on, by another bright ball. It wasn't so forgiving. It swallowed his vessel whole and left nothing behind. Neither plasma nor fighter remained.

Her pride, her elation from seconds ago was torn away while she watched, powerless. It was over. Her energy ebbed away with each thought.

No.

She wanted to scream the word, but what was the point?

No.

Loss. Anger. Hate. Revenge. They all burned brighter but shorter than a flaring match.

No.

Why go on? Why? She flew on in a straight line, numb to the subtle variances of the assisted navigation. Numb to the calls from her speaker to change course. Numb to the thought that her own life could be taken just as remorselessly.

No.

All this death. All this loss. All her fault. She'd told the *Queen*. And she'd done it so eagerly.

No.

She looked up to see their destroyer pound some ship or other. She watched. Empty. This was their revenge, not hers. Jason was gone now and she'd be gone soon enough.

No.

She didn't want to die. But she didn't want to live this life, anymore.

No.

A voice interrupted her thoughts.

"Sally, are you all right? Were you hit?"

It was his voice. He was alive. Somehow. But she'd seen his red fighter erased by a ball of light. Blood and metal melted away and you could be forgiven for thinking it had never existed. Wait, was it Jason or a copy of his voice? She reconsidered that thought, then replaced it with: 'there is some advanced technology here'. Could a voice be copied?

"Where did you pick up the matches?"

A pause.

"Look, it was an accident. I didn't mean to take them."

There was a small measure of relief. Sufficient to fill a thimble. His voice again. It was concerned.

"What happened to you? You were right behind me, then you nearly overtook me but carried on in a straight line."

She built up the energy to speak. It took her two goes to be heard.

"I just saw you die. I was flying behind you and your ship was wiped away by one of those balls of light. I'd lost you and, somehow, you're back."

If Jason responded she didn't hear it, so she carried on.

"It's all gone wrong and I don't know how to make it right. We came here to find out what happened to Simon and now look. It's all my fault."

The voice cut in. It was tired, if a little surprised.

"Your fault? It's a little much to say you're responsible for a war."

"Minutes before you landed, I learned a terrible secret. Between us going downstairs that first time and now, I gave up the secret of this building to the very person who is now in charge. I was shown the exchange I had with her. It was me talking but I have no memory of it. They somehow erased my memories of that and who knows what else."

She was aware of a fighter flying alongside her. The readouts, the face behind the helmet, confirmed it was his ship. He turned, slightly and she followed. When the path straightened, they were heading to their destroyer.

"We always worried we might be caught and handed over to the police or, worse, to my parents. Instead, when they found us, they did something to us."

"What can we do? Can we find out what happened and undo it?" he asked.

"Can you become the Jason I knew yesterday? Can you undo

that?"

She gave the questions time to do their own work in the silence.

"The powers that be aren't going to be generous, all of a sudden. There's as much chance as the aliens switching the field into reverse for one human."

She said one more thing.

♟♝♚♛♝♟

Jason reflected on the previous minutes of his life. They'd no sooner dealt with the double triangle ship than another force had swept up behind. He wasn't sure who was supposed to have been watching the tracking. Perhaps all of them. On his first flight, that role had been his. The battle had waged so long that squads weren't made up by specialists, they were all survivors. Skill, with a good dollop of luck thrown in. There was no point in wasting time on pointing fingers, there were other things to focus on.

Sally was still behind him and there were fighters behind her. A burst of plasma fire came in from his right. Confused, he shifted the stick to his left. He anticipated the manoeuvre to turn him away and lower his trajectory. Instead, he rotated anticlockwise. He had his moment of luck. The shot could have removed a significant portion of one of the three thrust cylinders. Instead, it grazed the paintwork as he turned. He was alive, another survivor. Another burst of white light issued from the newest enemy ship. He felt the heat. Instinct forced his eyes shut. When he opened them again, he was fine. The shot must have missed by millimetres.

Repair systems had done a fine job fixing up the damage. Sally had drifted out of formation but one of the others was trying to bring her back in. Not *one* of the other fighters, he realised. It was the only other one. They had lost two, in that engagement. When he had her talking again, she had seen something.

"I don't know what you saw but I'm here."

Sally's words echoed in his head. He didn't know about those in charge but she sounded pretty certain about it. She'd been there. He hadn't.

Her voice sounded sapped of its spirit and he noticed the same drain in his own self. Looking down at himself, that was probably no bad thing. Throw the curveball of anxiety into this messy situation and it would amplify the problems. In any case, he couldn't go home in this state. Which dad would believe their boy had grown up so fast? He was very much alive but, equally, a casualty of war.

When Sally had uttered those three little words, he found no resistance in his heart. It wasn't that it was a good idea, it was that there weren't any better choices.

"Die with me," she had said.

The prospect of ending it all didn't fill him with dread. It neither filled nor emptied him. It was just an option. It didn't matter how but he decided that they should make an impact, somewhere. That would be a challenge. They could take out gun emplacements but, in terms of taking on a large ship, it was too much, for them.

They'd come here for Simon, to find a way to save him. At each attempt, they'd not just failed but made things worse. One part of him said they shouldn't give up. Another said, could we make this worse? How could this be worse? That he couldn't think of an answer didn't fill him with any positivity. He hadn't envisioned a war yet here he was, in the middle of one. He couldn't imagine being exposed to that smog but Simon had. He and Sally hatched the plan to pump some of the medicine from the floor into their friend. Assuming they could get hold of it and the hospital would allow them to apply it to them. It was optimistic to believe whatever they picked up would be the answer. It could make him worse. Jason didn't recall all the attention being directed at the woman lying on the floor was going to save her. He could hear it in the desperation of the voices of her colleagues. Jason believed he couldn't save his friend. Some of this was his fault but he felt he was fighting someone else's battle. He'd lost himself in that green field. Even if he hadn't aged and gone home after all this, what would he be taking back? Who was he? He'd seen so much. He almost welcomed the absence of feelings. They protected him.

He looked around. Finally, there was a down, a relative point. He could see the Earth. It was so small he could eclipse it with the tip of his little finger. He couldn't make out the moon or any continents but it was there. The only thing he was sure of was that that he wanted to protect his home.

He scanned the tracker and saw the immense ship, protected by cruisers, destroyers and fighters. Too large for them, perhaps? Something always made it through, didn't it? The attacking force had been damaged along the way but were pressing for a final assault on his little blue planet. Were they going to bomb from above or drop troops to the surface? Either way, they were invaders. Such a force wouldn't expect a small squad of fighters to attack. That was one thing in their favour.

There was no return ticket for his journey. Not a normal advantage to crow about. But if you press an attack, you also need to consider a route out, as well as in. He closed his eyes. When he reached a decision, he nodded and spoke.

"Let's end this. You and me."

He put out a call, summoning all fighters. They needed support. They had a daring target, worthy of this fighting force. He called to the remaining fighter, behind him and advised it to stay sharp. Sally formed up behind him and to his right, with the third taking rear left. He instructed them to select passive tracking, to minimise visibility. He chose an approach route that matched the shape of an elongated 'S' on three axes. When they were close, they would go straight in. The protected ship had a bulbous shape at the front.

As the second extended curve of the 'S' neared its conclusion, Jason checked the tracker. He identified upwards of thirty enemy fighters, heading their way. Too many. More radar colours radiated from further afield. He maintained his approach and offered a determined face.

"Make yourself as visible on your radars as much as possible while we take a new route, away from their fighters."

The enemy force adjusted their own attack formation to intercept him. They would meet each other in ten seconds. His eyes flickered between the approaching groups. It was going to be tight. He issued a short instruction to the pair behind.

Two seconds before they engaged, the three rotated up and hit full speed. The enemy were all neatly lined up, with their focus away from the second group: twenty Earth fighters, answering his call. The enemy fighters were caught in a moment of indecision between attacking the three ahead against turning to face the new threat. Trying to do both created confusion. The engagement quickly went the way of the home team and allowed the three to change back to their route and continue onward. It shattered the resolve of the alien force enough that a number of fighters survived and joined Jason's charge. In amongst the outer line of picket ships, batteries fired frantically.

More Earth fighters joined from the other side of this fleet. They took valuable attention away from his group. More fighters but, also, more enemy ships were arriving. Jason wondered where the larger ships were. The fighters couldn't just turn up, without them. He checked the mirror again. Sally and the others were still on his left and right quarters. Her voice came over the speakers.

"These ships can self-heal by moving parts around?"

"Yes."

"Enough to adjust the shapes and look like the enemy?" she enquired.

There was a pause before Jason confirmed the outside was fluid but the structure was not. It could be reshaped but not enough to look so different, the enemy would stop shooting at them.

As Jason neared the large ship, he drew the focus of more of weapons fire, the level of explosions increased. He fought to control his direction. He turned and twisted to avoid the worst of the harm sent his way. One of the explosions went off right next to him and wedged a slice of material into a thruster. He felt the impact as one of the ports was jammed open. Whenever he tried to change direction, his movement wasn't quite as expected.

Barrages of flak and energy pulses were sent out to intercept him and block off the area into which he might manoeuvre. Red lights flashed the bad news. The afterburners lit up and fuel was thrown out the back of the fighter to increase his speed. The dented rear of the ship directed the fierce burn behind him and he felt the straps bite into his ribs. Plasma fire passed and flak detonated in empty space as he veered away, on a tangent.

It was hard to feel like he was there. There was no air to carry the sound to him. Explosions might as well have been millions of miles away. Even when he was hit, the impact felt so minimal. There was a metallic rain on the canopy and vibrations caused by the engine. If not for them, he might not think he was there.

Computer-controlled ships flew against computer-controlled guns. It came down to whichever was the best. Before this battle, Earth's were ahead. Centuries of collaboration in the galactic empire shared wondrous technologies. The squadrons found the attacking force had upgraded their trackers when they approached to short range. Losses were high.

The tracking on Jason's visor told him the sphere ship's speed was decreasing. His computer estimated it would end up in a position in orbit over the north-pole in around thirty minutes. He fought for control and his ship veered off his chosen path at each correction. Speed and manoeuvrability were reduced and incoming fire was becoming problematic. He had known it was going to be hard and he'd done well to make it this far, but getting closer was proving to be impossible.

This situation was an ever-decreasing spiral of luck and resources. His versus the enemy's. Periodically, groups of three and more peeled off. After a few seconds, they rejoined. The scope indicated twenty-five fighters, other than his.

The large ship could have been a lollipop or a match. He couldn't advance on it with its defensive fire. Around them was a selection of misshapen cruisers and other ships. A voice on the wire said those few not firing were landing ships.

"They have to clear us out of the way before they would land their troops."

Sally dialled in on a private line to say she wasn't so sure. They'd seen the Earth destroyed. No one's going to put down troops and then blow up the planet they're on.

Either way, they hadn't much time to act before something happened. He needed to move in close and run some scans. A mile out, the flak screen of coloured eruptions became intensive and he pulled back. As he tried to manoeuvre again, the jammed thruster sent him through the wall between explosions. He took advantage.

Nothing appeared to be happening. Incoming fire hadn't eased but there weren't any of the explosions. It didn't make sense until Sally picked a possible solution.

"They kind of guess where you are. The wall of fire is simple desperation but it's enough to keep out fighters. I think it's the minimum range of their guns. Once you're through they can't hit you in the same way. The guns are still firing but we're inside where they would explode."

Sally's voice sounded disjointed, far away. That was enough of a push for the enlarged squad to penetrate the shield. The fighters moved in to attack its defensive weapons. Jason was taken over by a lethargy. All urgency in pressing the attack slipped away.

A loud crackling sound burst onto his speakers, deafening him, momentarily. The transmission came through with a deep, gargling sound. It accompanied the crackling, for a few seconds then the noise ended, abruptly. A translation shortly arrived over the wire.

"Your overtures of peace have been acknowledged for their deception. Your war-hungry species will soon be removed from this galaxy. Its remnants will be hunted down and exterminated as a message that will echo, forever. We came here seeking your surrender but reports from our home planets indicate you are without integrity. The Empire was once great and your species rightly took its place at the centre. Your ingenuity was unrivalled. But now, too much has been lost to sponsor your existence."

The signal ended.

"What the hell? Had someone been negotiating a truce, after all this? Shouldn't we have been told?" exclaimed Sally.

There was nothing Jason could say. He was distracted when his ship detected multiple launch warnings. Rockets blasted and blurred out from tubes at the front of six of the ships around him. Alarm bells rang and shifted from self-preservation to relief to guilt. He thought he was the target, then realised it was Earth. Orbital defences intercepted the bulk of these on approach and after. Then the ships focused energy fire on the platforms, after which all the missiles passed through. Information uploaded into his visor updated him that each missile had multiple warheads, that would eradicate cities from the map. The numbers of missiles did not abate and even the existence of the map was in jeopardy.

A cheer had gone up when similar actions had been taken by Earth's ships against the enemy's worlds. They now felt the impact for themselves. Not all of those watching had been born on Earth, yet it was their ancestral home and they were fiercely loyal to it. Some of the fighters began firing at the launchers. This left them close to static for single turrets and flak batteries, and easier to track. One drifted right in front of the tubes, as it tried to disable it. The next launch drove straight through the fighter, destroying it and the pilot. The missile carried on towards the surface.

Jason fell into a state of rolling with the punches of the defensive fire. He stared at the destruction. He had a sort-of plan when he approached the ships and had allowed himself to be distracted from it. But now, the future of Earth depended upon the plan being carried out. It wasn't enough to dodge the fire and maybe shoot up a few turrets. He would have to attack the cruisers at their weak points. Except, they didn't have any that a fighter could exploit. His experiences to date had informed him that these little fighters were there for taking out small targets. One little fighter wasn't going to break through the hull of these vessels, not without help. And where was that help? Fighters continued to join them, yet the ships that had the firepower were not to be found.

He had summoned a stack of freelancers to come and fight for him. Meanwhile, he wasn't doing much more than skim over the surface of this ship to stop it and others firing at him. He had forgotten why he was there. Within a few seconds, it came back to him. Then he was under attack.

This time, two turrets were firing at him from different places. In the moment, he figured out that pushing down was the only guaranteed move, so a quick half-rotation and the lollipop was above him. He pushed down, rotated, stretching his forearm, then pushed it to evade, going back the way he came. When the thought returned to him, he suspected his brain was distracting him.

It knows what I want to do. Maybe it's trying to protect itself from me.

Tracking had picked up enough data to present a wire picture of the ship. It lit up critical systems, including energy stores. There was a weak point, right in the middle of the lollipop stick. There was only one option. Sally's voice cut through into his world.

"There's no way we can go home now. By the time we did, the building would be flattened."

He made the decision again. He was properly out of options now. Weapons fire glanced off his hull and brought his mind back to the present. He had been watching the impossible. It was time to find out what was possible.

"Computer, what kind of power unit is on this ship?"

A ticker tape of text began scrolling across his view.

"Can you respond in speech? I don't have the opportunity to read, right now."

A slightly tinny male voice responded.

"The vessel is powered by a *Continuum Enterprises Mark Three* power fusion cell. It is capable of maintaining life support, engines, weapons and monitoring all residual systems for up to a twelve-hour combat period. *Continuum Enterprises* are the landmark in progressive aero-spatial engineering—"

"Yes, yes, all right. Enough of the sales brochure."

Passing shells sped above him, then one struck and cracked the screen above his head. He flinched and the stick dropped enough to push him out of immediate danger. He pushed it forward and, once again, took off at a tangent. The crack healed itself as he swept around the circumference of the lollipop. Another three missiles launched right in front of him. He tried again.

"Is there enough power in the reactor to energise weapons to crack the hull?" he asked.

"There is insufficient energy in the power unit for weapons to effect damage to breach the outer hull," replied the tinny voice.

"What happens if you divert all power from available systems apart from navigation and life support to the weapons?" offered Jason, with a sliver hope in his voice.

"There is insufficient energy remaining in the power unit."

He found it odd that he was viewing this entirely as a puzzle.

"What do I need to do to blow up the reactor?"

"There are safety protocols in place to prevent overload."

"Can they be overridden? I am the pilot. This is my decision. I want to override them."

No response. He wondered if he'd asked the wrong question.

"Safeties have been removed," came the reply, after a pause. "The core will feedback for sixty seconds, when it will detonate."

Jason's breath quickened. There was no avoiding it.

"At what point will radiation become terminal?"

No hesitation from the system. "Terminal levels occurred once the safeties were removed."

That was that, then. The decision had been made. He felt pinpricks in his back. Pins and needles, one last time. The information about the radiation would be right. He had no reason to doubt it. It was likely the radiation was not so much pricking the skin as puncturing his organs. Less than a second passed before he relayed a message and his method to the other fighters. He was surprised that Sally hadn't challenged it. She only said she would follow him in.

"To make sure."

It was the second to last thing she said to him.

The little fighters with elevated power from their reactors were moving much faster now and were harder to hit. Skimming over the surface of the ships protected them. The cruisers continued firing their missiles as more of their ships moved into the battle area.

Jason requested an internal schematic view be overlaid when he looked at the enemy. This enabled him to view the vulnerable areas. Half a dozen key systems were buried just under the surface. He wondered what kind of energy release would be required to access them. He hadn't realised he'd been talking out loud, when he received the 'insufficient information' response. He guessed it had never been done before.

Now he was free. It was an odd phrase but, for less than a minute, he could play with the fighter. Now it was a flying ship, rather than a combat ship. He had an appointment with the long ship in forty-three seconds but that was an issue for future Jason. Earth looked amazing, from here. Bright flashes emanated from the surface, followed by clouds. They might not know his name, down there but he thought of them. He thought of the next city that would be hit.

The supercharged power core was moving him faster. He decided where he was going to meet the ship and fired at three turrets in that area. Between weaving moves, he poured in his ammunition at each, putting them beyond use. They probably had some self-repair process but he doubted they could fix themselves, in time.

Cracks appeared in his screen from flak, near and far. They were no longer being repaired. He turned off the auto-repair to focus on delivering the vital punch. A ball of deep blue plasma tore past his ship underneath and its heat seared the hull of the fighter. It melted a hole beneath him. The cockpit depressurised and the temperature began to drop. Systems compensated by sending more heat through his suit. Jason pressed himself against the seat to absorb the warmth from the overloading engine.

Another fighter shot past him, as they crossed at their elevated speeds. Jason activated a power screen to see where the energy levels were. The needle was as high as it could go. He asked for a visual countdown to explosion.

Fourteen seconds. He switched his microphone permanently on so the others would know what he was doing. He ordered the computer to detonate when his fighter struck the ship, to ensure maximum damage.

Ten seconds. He was facing away from his target but that was the plan. He lifted the stick up, tilted the top towards his chest and looped around. He knew he'd never see home again. He looked to the right and upon his old friend, the Sun, then down to the blue planet for one last time. He had to lean forward, into the cold, as the heat from behind his chair was becoming unbearable.

That guttural voice came through the speakers, followed shortly by a translation.

"We can help you. We can change you back. Make you young again. You need to come closer."

Was it true? Was it imagined? Come closer? Was it a bluff? He shook his head. It must be a last, desperate lie to change his mind. It was too late. The radiation was terminal. He looked forward. The end was in sight. The turrets were still down. Three seconds.

Sally's voice came over the speakers. He spotted her speedy fighter completing its loop and levelling off, behind him.

"I love you."

He repeated the words back to her. He didn't feel it. He didn't feel at all.

One second. He relaxed his grip on the stick and his eyes stayed open to the last, where instinct took over. His small craft struck the enemy hull, a few feet from where he'd been aiming.

He didn't feel the impact when his fighter, at full burn, slammed into the long ship.

Zero. A bright light filled his cockpit and the explosion tore through the side of the ship. Jason didn't feel the accompanying explosion from the fighter's core. It wasn't enough to destroy it but it had made a large hole in the side.

Sally had followed him everywhere, sometimes in spirit. She had been behind him when he and Simon had run to the building. Had he been embarrassed? Simon had noticed it, too. They were pretty confident Jason liked her. The offered her a way out. An escape. She'd been in front of Jason in the run from the guards. Now she was behind him. She hadn't wanted to be here. She couldn't go home. Not now. Not after all this. She couldn't have him, only to see him taken away. There was no longer a way out. It wasn't what she wanted but it was all that was left.

Sally didn't exactly follow his route, in case the enemy fire picked them both up. The ship was interfering in its own way and the movements were adding to her discombobulation. Moving downwards gave her nausea. She had instructed the system to generate a projected flight path onto her visor. This would enable her to be aware of every twist and turn. It beat the churn of being thrown left and right, unexpectedly.

Jason was ahead of her. Who was he now? She had a house to return to but she didn't want to go there. Someone once wrote, 'We get the families we deserve.' She wondered if they had a complaints department.

The time on her display measured in seconds and it dropped into single digits. She was scared. Scared of dying. Scared of the unknown. The church said Saint Peter was waiting on the other side and her relatives would have to pray her into heaven. How would that work, if no one knew she was dead, or if everyone who knew her had died a million years before?

Jason had levelled off. This was it. The energy signature of his fighter lit up like a Christmas tree. The long ship wasn't firing at him. Perhaps it knew, somehow, that the end was coming, whatever it did. Had the captain looked out of a window to see two tonnes of bricks falling towards the ship? Had they known there was nothing that could stop it?

To herself, Sally said goodbye to Jason, as the seconds counted down. She activated the chat and told him she loved him. And she did. In the last moments of her life, she was free to express herself.

The warmth on her back told her she wouldn't survive, even if she ejected now. Who would save her, out here? The invaders had been clear that they were here to exterminate all humans. Ejecting would only make their task easier.

Jason spoke to her as his little fighter headed into the colossal structure. Even on the extended cylinder, the diameter was maybe five times the height of their church on the hill. The bubble at the front was easily double that. The signal wave from his fighter flat-lined a split second before the explosion. Now it was her turn. The light brigade had done the hard part. Now it was the turn of the heavy brigade to follow up and make it count.

The controls fought her to avoid the impact. It wasn't enough to say she was going to die. She had to want to die in each moment. To see it through right to the end. She had to fight against the ship for the right to die. There was so much death here. All the zero jumps tearing up lives. Should the ship not understand what was happening? Did she have to pull the trigger as well as point the gun at her head?

There was a hole in the ship and she was going in. Despite the heat on her back, her body felt cold. With her heart and mind at the point of overload, she pulled the trigger and flew into the hole Jason had made for her.

The fighter penetrated the hull just shy of full speed and

clipped debris and shattered walls. The momentum of Sally's fighter was preceded by the extending bow wave of pressure from the previous exploding fighter. It was enough to penetrate through to the energy store. Metal scraped and scored the hull of the flimsy vessel as it broke through the collapsing structure. Twenty feet in and the cockpit was crushed beyond recognition. The engine's core was a solid lump and in the last throes of a feedback loop. The remnants of the fighter were stopped by the dent it put in the otherwise solid wall, protecting the energy storage. When it stopped, there was no life inside. Sally's engine went critical as it touched the energy store. Light. Heat. Her fighter became the detonator for a vast bomb.

Despite the massive size of the ship, the explosion killed it. The fighter had made it through. Power failed, life support and gravity stopped. The long ship broke in two. Its own momentum, coupled with Earth's gravity, drew it towards the atmosphere. The bulk would burn up, before crashing in the nuclear wasteland made by its cohorts.

Following their example, the remaining enlarged squadron that had answered Jason's call to arms removed other ships. They created their own tribute to the zero jump. Not all the ships were removed from action and the missiles kept launching.

CHAPTER 11

Sally was in darkness, shocked by the bright light that appeared ahead. She had to shield her eyes. She was still aware of herself. There was a sensation of shaking. There was a presence. It touched her physically. She felt a hand on her shoulder. She felt a release and the pressure on her relaxed. The light dimmed a little, as her eyes adjusted. She heard a voice.

"Are you alright?"

The shaking returned. It seemed distant somehow. The voice spoke again.

"There was no way to know."

It was the fresh air that brought her round. She blinked back the tears several times and adjusted to the light, shielding her eyes as she did. The voice belonged to Jason. Jason, the man. Her straps had been removed. She sat up and looked around. They were exactly where they'd taken off. He spoke again.

"I'm sorry. I didn't know. They looked the same."

The ground shook again, more strongly, this time.

Still nervous from the recent experience, she stuttered out a question.

"What happened?"

"Simulators."

She looked at his face. A face of a life avoided, that he would now have to endure. Except his eyes betrayed no emotion.

"Was it all a lie?"

He explained they been flying remotely.

"The fighters were real and the damage we did was done."

"But we were here, all along?"

Jason nodded.

"It was why the green zone had no effect on you. The radiation in the engine won't harm us. It was an immersive simulator, designed to look and feel like the real thing. If our fighters were lost, we would be moved to control the nearest empty one. Maybe that's what you saw."

Without a word, she scrabbled and scrambled out, then hugged him. The ground shook again. They both had to put a hand on the lookalike fighter for support. She looked up at him, questioningly.

"The information on the computer says missiles are still impacting the ground. We can't stay here. The missiles will finish us, for sure."

She could ask more questions but she didn't want to complicate things further. Jason carried on with the previous subject.

"Not all the strikes are on the surface. A few missiles tunnel into the ground. They're destroying the planet's surface and structure. We need to move."

Seconds later, they found themselves running towards the building again. They weren't under direct fire, this time but it wouldn't be any easier. Each shake of the ground made their steps falter and bodies fall. Sally clung to the grass as though she might hold on to it by the might of her own will. Each quake lasted seconds. The walkway appeared unmoved and undamaged but she preferred the sanctity of grass.

There was a flicker of light over the horizon. The missiles were coming. In the building, there was enough power to see by. It was the backstage to the television show. Out front was all the lights, the magic and the sensation. Behind the set were unswept floors, bare wires and spiders' webs. There weren't any of that here but it looked so dingy. Most of the lights were off or damaged and there was a sense that the staff and equipment had been evacuated.

Sally led anticlockwise around to the inner sanctum and was grateful not to see the bad aunt again. She turned the last corner to see a short, open corridor, leading to the large room. No trickery with the walls, this time. Inside, two figures remained. The Queen was dressed, if that was the right word, in her sparkling, light blue regalia. She stood facing her Knight. Sally thought he was leaving it a bit late to escape. He might be caught up in the blast. A just reward for an unjust man.

Another quake ran through the ground. Windows cracked with the shaking. Buildings in the distance toppled but the building they were in absorbed it all. The building's owners were looking at screens.

"Look at all the pawns *Black* has brought to play, today. Our task is almost complete," mused Knight.

"Here come our heroes. Back from the front," said his Queen.

Looking at Jason, she laughed – or issued what she might have thought was a laugh.

"Don't they grow up fast, these days?" she said to Knight. Then, to Jason and Sally, she continued, "We have an important job for you. Can you take on the role of planetary custodians? It won't trouble you for long, I assure you."

"You're sick," replied Sally.

"Remind me again; is that good or bad?" Knight retorted.

"You've destroyed everything. The planet, the fleet, killed all the pilots and yourselves. For what?" asked Jason.

"Mr Sumner," replied Knight, "it is fine. It was all a gamble that paid off. This planet is, indeed, doomed. It was doomed from the beginning. We simply adjusted our plans and moved to a second home. A new Earth, if you will. Do you know how hard it is to find a temperate planet with an iron core? Humanity has been living there for some time. The fleet may look scattered but most of it is around our new home. The rest are doing to the aliens' homes what they're about to do to yours. Once they are done up there, where do you think they're going to go? They no longer have homes – or, rather, not homes as they would have hoped. The irony is that it was the fate they had in store for us. They were certain we'd be hunted down, ship by ship, but it will be them."

There was an air of disdain emanating from his lips that made Sally feel sick.

"You're going to destroy the Earth," Sally said, voicing Jason's thought.

"No," replied Knight. "They will, but I take your point. We knew, from the beginning, that any action taken against the greater Alliance would result in the destruction of Earth. We used that to our advantage. You see, they're a bit black and white. They couldn't see the big picture. Our hit and run tactics annoyed them, time and time again and forced them to stop the problem at its source. And so, they deployed a vast invasion fleet. Except, even that is a lie. It is bigger than it should be and contains merchantmen and farm ships. To make them look bigger. Do you know what that means?"

Sally simply stared. He would carry on regardless of whatever she said or did. It was Jason who replied.

"They've overcommitted."

Knight was delighted. "Precisely. Our ships met little resistance at their worlds. We started this war to restore balance to the galaxy. Instead, thanks to you, we will become its overlords. We will not just beat them but beat them down. This place," he looked up and around, "has served us well. It will deliver us from the ruins of an existence into the supreme beings of our time."

Oh my God, thought Sally.

She was glad she didn't say it out loud. Knight could think she was praising him. There was no doubt in his eyes. This wasn't about something that was going to happen. It had happened. This was all about going through the motions to make it a reality.

"There isn't time. The evacuation isn't complete," she pointed out.

Knight was pleased to inform her that her information was incorrect. The planet was mostly clear, apart from those who wouldn't leave and those they didn't want.

"They are, even now, wandering the vacated streets or clinging to each other in their homes, feeling and fearing the quakes. The streets have been emptied of more than just people. We have moved house and made *New Earth* look like a home from home. We haven't just burned our bridges with the Alliance, we have burned our boats with the old planet."

Another tremor passed through the floor. It shook both Sally and Jason but not the other two. Jason took that moment to remind Sally they should leave, soon. Sally imagined it would be impossible for anyone to flee now. She was almost triumphant that Knight was trapped and indicated as much.

"Doesn't that leave you a bit exposed, being here?"

"My dear," he replied, "I am already in our new home. What you see of me is simply a projection."

She tried to compare the respective appearances of him and Victoria.

"She has been moving round various locations and needs to occupy a lower bandwidth to enable that. Therefore, she looks less human. Also, she is in the machine and soon, I will be too."

"Earth has lost," Sally said disconsolately.

"Yet, Earth has also won. One minus one equals one."

"Earth started the war," continued Sally.

"And now, through their overconfidence, the Alliance has allowed us to finish it. Humanity will live on. *New Earth* is already two billion strong. You know, it was we who invented jump space or, rather, discovered it. Create a little gravity well, fly into it and repeat until you reach your destination. We gave that up and still crawled into the Alliance. It was more of a commercial venture than a militaristic one, but the exchange of money smoothed over the cracks. Big companies were made more powerful, until you had their bosses driving the agenda. Governments kowtowed to their whims. Policy should not be made that way. We're looking to reset a few things."

"Why give up the Earth?" Sally made herself heard.

"Because they wanted it. Because they wanted to show us who was boss. To show how wrong we were. Reserves have been held aside, to stop some of their more interesting plans, such as sending nearby stars into nova. You spotted that one. It would have been close enough to destroy all the planets in our system, plus Sol. So, we sent ships to eradicate their construction sites and cities. We won't knock them back to the Stone Age, though they might wish for a simpler life, after today.

"*New Earth* won't be made from inherited land, old money or those personalities. It will be peopled by migrants, all looking for a new life. Keen to make a good impression and rebuild society, the way it should be. There will be a little readjustment to the bacteria and other interesting life forms but that's nothing new, for us. We will adapt. Technology, coupled with land and air reformers, has already responded well. Importantly, they will be in possession of a lot of anger at those who destroyed their homes here. It's a perfect arrangement, I think you'll agree.

"This ball here, was central to the whole thing. The engineers created it as the first step to the gravity drives. They are commonplace, as you have both experienced it. This first one included something that has never been replicated. Time manipulation. Apparently, it was damaged at some point and its energies diverted along a different path. If it hadn't been for you two and your friend, we would never have known. Humanity will rule from the centre of the board. The other races will, in time, return to the stars where they will find us waiting for them."

"You won't win, you know," Sally kept going out of sheer bloody-mindedness.

"Excuse me? How on Earth, what's left of it, can you say that?"

"All empires end. The longer they expect to last, the shorter they do. You won't see out the year."

"My conversion will take place, soon enough. I will join with the machine and ascend with the Queen who went before me."

"The enemy will be back."

"An optimist. You're a rare breed. The best optimistic forecast puts the first defeated race into the stars in a little over two hundred years. I think we'll be fine, but thank you for your concern. Every last drop of it. Your work here is done. You may go."

"And we will rule," said Victoria, finally breaking her silence.

"Until the power runs out," Sally pointed out, rallying.

"That is unlikely," Knight responded.

His eyes sparkled with a delight that continued to annoy her. She wanted to find something to get back at him for everything they'd done. For Jason, for the people they'd kidnapped and stuffed in those tubes, for her and for Simon.

"You're not leading the world. You're herding sheep. Oh, does that hurt? Not such a great leader, more a herdsman. Maybe not now or tomorrow but, eventually, someone will smell a rat and come for you. The undesirables have been left behind and it won't take long for some to realise who, then why."

"Our guards keep us safe," he responded in his snootiest

manner.

"And they're the ones you'll have to watch more closely. They have the access."

"You're just being paranoid."

And now, you are. The seeds of doubt have been sown.

"Your comments have no grounding in reality." Knight continued.

"Reliance on technology is another. You may be the brightest and the best in the galaxy but not because you're better. It's because you destroyed the opposition. What happens when a greater power comes from outside the galaxy? What if you could only have beaten them with the forces you have just annihilated? Earth's firepower would have won many plaudits in its defence."

At last, silence from the man who could be a herder. He was about to speak when Sally delivered one last line.

"And what if they are watching, even now? At last, able to step in and take this galaxy at the point where there is no fight left in it?"

"That's even more wishful thinking," Knight retorted, but his face betrayed doubt. He looked at Victoria and both their images ceased projecting.

Sally set off but Jason called to her.

"We've left the building and I can't say I want to run around outside, to only climb back in where we're standing."

She stopped with two heavy, braking feet.

"Maybe it's enough to touch the window or that ball?"

"I want to touch that ball even less than I want to go outside."

A powerful rumble shook the building back and forth. Where there had been one long wall, either side of the large room became fragmented into numerous rectangular shapes. The building seemed set to tear itself apart around them. A blast wave tore through the newly formed shapes. Glass showered down on them.

When the earthquake subsided enough for them to try and stand, Sally rose carefully, so any glass resting on her skin wouldn't cut her. She began to shimmy, in the manner of a dog shaking off surplus water. Through the window, her eyes caught something moving in the distance and she stopped. A large mushroom was growing into the sky.

"Jason," she whimpered.

His eyes followed hers, then he spoke.

"One chance only. Touch the frame now and run back to the stairs. Don't look back."

She touched first and ran from the room. He overtook her on the way round. She kept him in sight as they bolted round the corridors, the way they'd snuck in. She saw him cut through where the inner door had been. As she stepped into the foyer, another mushroom cloud rose up in the distance. To her right, Jason was hanging by his fingers from the third step from the top. All the other stairs below were missing. Underneath was an all-consuming void. She touched her belt, unconsciously. The end was close. If there had been any steps down, they were gone, lost to the tremors and the void. It wasn't easy to tell if the frame had done what was needed. If she jumped, she might be able to reach him from here, but could she hang on to him? Could his fingers hold both of them?

♟♟♙♙♙♟

Jason's new fingers were stronger but his body was heavier. He knew what was below and didn't dare look. If he slipped, he would never know. He was using all his energy to hang on. He could feel the tiredness in his muscles, as his body sagged under the stress. As his feet dangled near the rising black tide, his toes found something firm. Then he was on solid ground. Both he and

Sally were standing on a large, white tile.

"Still rushing in ahead of the angels?" She smiled.

They both alighted from the tile to the step above the one he'd been clinging to and into the most explosive, electrically charged landing they'd seen. Jagged lightning bolts left ominously deep red walls, floors and ceiling. Each one stung wherever they touched. The cold, the strikes and next, the pins and needles. Jason felt he was being herded forward and rejected. He extended a hand to her and the pair turned upstairs, holding on to each other.

CHAPTER 12

Fresh air touched Jason's face. It smelled like home.

They emerged from the door years too early. They'd gone up a few flights to offset their future travels and overcompensated. A further complication was that, upon opening the door, they found no bin. There was one at the tree line, between the stiles and Jason jogged out, hoping to find a newspaper with evidence of a date. The next trip out overcompensated too far the other way and Jason foresaw a problem. Up and down and out and back. In another time, one could develop a fitness regime, through this.

"I have an idea that will help a little," he offered.

Two hours later and a couple of years earlier, they peered out and saw the builder's hut was back. The scaffolding wasn't yet erected and they spotted a couple of workmen. They waited inside for an opportunity. It was an odd experience to have the men poking around, sometimes right outside the door but unaware they were being watched. Sally was impatient about the delay. As the sun dipped down on the other side of the building, the shadows lengthened away towards the hut. A rain cloud produced a scattering of heavy showers and a scampering of men inside. They closed their toolboxes but left them unlocked. Seconds after they closed their door, Jason opened his and bolted towards a corner of the temporary office. He moved so he would be less visible to them. Peering inside, he could see that one man was obscured by the other, who had his back to the window. Jason opened the toolbox and relieved it of a small item that wouldn't be missed, then shut the lid. He returned to the corner of the hut to find them absent from view. They could be just about to leave. He took a chance, circled back and returned to the building, holding the pliers.

It isn't theft. It's borrowing, he thought. *I'll return it soon enough.*

He led Sally up to the landing. It was enough to trigger the aggressive flashes, then he returned to the floor and stepped back out into a winter's evening. There was barely any light, which worked well for the activity but not for finding his way there or cutting the retainers. He didn't see anyone out and about, at this hour. Once the bin was separated from its secure resting place, he returned it to the place just outside the door, where they'd been used to seeing it. As they, once again, began fine-tuning their return, they noticed a footpath being worn into the grass. The locals were diverted from their usual route.

Backwards and forwards, then back again. Trips up and down, out and back began to take their toll on Jason's gallant attitude. As tiredness worked into his muscles and their energy, Sally put her foot down. She told him to stay inside. Each time the run out to check the papers and back to the building was taking longer. A crunch moment arrived when she returned, only to forget the date and had to go back. There were times when no paper availed itself of their needs and they had to try again. Jason noticed Sally's attention was fading. Her fanaticism to depart was affecting her focus. She banged her fist on the wall in frustration.

Slowly, through the tears, she uttered, "I just want to go home."

Finally, after hours of work, they arrived at a date that elated Sally. She rushed back to the foyer. He'd asked her the date and she'd responded with a frustrating, "Guess, guess!" There was a renewed fervour in her purpose. It was written in the tape, flapping in the breeze from the scaffolding. Except, something was missing. Jason realised it couldn't be the date he had expected when the tape flapping from the scaffolding was only the red one. It didn't include the one left by the police. He found a bin to hold open the door and headed towards her. He checked the date on the coffee-stained paper in the bin. It was the day Simon didn't come home. Still holding the paper, he looked back at her. She was delirious. She explained this was the opportunity to right the wrongs.

"To show those arseholes we can stop this thing."

The sun came out from behind a cloud and the angle of the shadow indicated to Jason it was late morning. It would be a few hours before the three of them showed up.

Behind her delight, Sally looked drained from all the time it had taken to reach even here. He might almost say she was unwell. Neither of them had any money. Food wasn't available and he didn't know when it would be. Almost immediately after that thought, his stomach began talking to him. They both needed a good, warm meal in their bellies. In the absence of that, the next best thing was a long drink. It would help put some weight into their stomachs but it was unlikely that there was any drinking water. He was reluctant to drink from a wash basin as it might not be from the mains. In the absence of a choice, he led Sally to the Ladies and he awarded himself a visit to the Gents. He washed his hands for a long time to release more water from the tank. There wasn't much pressure in the taps and he suspected the tank wasn't being refilled. He decided to try his luck. What came out from the taps was clear but he closed his eyes as he drank it, as if not seeing would somehow make it cleaner.

He waited a long time for Sally to emerge. After a while, he sat down. He looked at how his fingers had changed. The moment he wanted to look at them, the material around them retreated to his wrists.

His nails were neatly manicured with pristine crescents. They hadn't looked like that since he could remember. His maturity had rendered a good form, physically. He wondered how much of it was down to his suit. He considered what control he might have over it.

Cover, he thought, and the material extended over his palm then along each of his fingers simultaneously.

He looked at the material that covered him from neck to toe. He thought a one-piece black outfit would look silly. The material was designed to keep him alive in a vacuum, so it would have to be incredibly durable. A memory, possibly an implanted one, told him it had the capacity to clean itself. Though functional, it just wasn't attractive.

Everyone will stare. As a test, he thought, *Could the top half be green, preferably the colour of freshly cut grass on a summer's day?*

A change in his peripheral vision drew his attention to the top half. The colour had changed to his definition upwards from where a belt may have been worn. He added colour to the arms, though it left his hands covered in the original black, in the cut of a waistcoat. It produced buttons up the middle at his request. He moved to the trousers and spent a good half an hour working it out for himself, then educating the material as to how denim should look and feel. During the time, he recalled the material recharged with sunlight.

There was a noise from within the Ladies that could have been a toilet flushing. Sally emerged, minutes later, looking no different. It didn't take Jason long to realise Sally wasn't well. Her concentration came and went. She started a sentence then stopped in the middle, as though someone had turned her off. She started talking again, as though nothing had happened.

"Don't you see... We can stop... this. We can stop it from...

ever happening. That's... good, isn't... it?"

What was going on? Was he doing the same thing but not noticing? He looked through the window at the flapping tape and there didn't appear to be any disconnect from one moment to another.

What if Simon has already gone? What if this was yesterday's paper? And what if the police were advancing on the building right now, about to add their colours to the scaffold?

"We... can undo... the mistake," she said.

"Stop him coming in at all? Should we stop him or explain it to him?" Jason asked.

"I'll... do... it."

"Why not me?"

"Would he... believe... you?"

He had to repeat himself. He doubted Sally's ability to explain a basic sentence to anyone, let alone this complicated mess. When she wasn't speaking, the pauses affected her movement. He looked around and didn't see anyone, not that it was a guarantee that no one was there. Although, who would stake out such a building? His thoughts were drawn to the man from the future but he was gone, wasn't he? Though his younger form could be here. Hadn't Sally seen a man when they first came here? He moved her round to the room at the back, in the open-plan office. There was a space between two desks, next to the slightly open window. He looked up and there was an entanglement of wires and small pipes. It was hard to see how to remove them from the window.

He kept a hand on Sally's shoulder to guide her and let her know where he was. He looked out, over the field. This was his home, until someone decided climbing into this building was a good idea. Somewhere out there, was his dad. He should have had a feeling towards him but none came. As his eyes scanned to the left, towards the tree line, he saw movement. It must be getting close to the time. He wanted to meet him here but, if Simon looked in before he climbed in, what might he think? Also, Jason knew what had driven Simon in. If Simon didn't come in, he didn't know what would happen outside, and he didn't want to see it. He reached out a hand for Sally. When he made no contact, he looked around, to see her lying on the floor. He moved and knelt beside her. She was alive and her eyes were open but not blinking. That looked odd and he tried to move her eyelids down. They immediately opened. Jason lifted her up, slightly then picked her up in his arms. He looked out the window and back to her.

Are you affected by the real Sally, just beyond the tree line? We've come back to her time. Your time is at least a week from now. But then, why am I not affected?

He carried her round to the corner and sat her down, next to the inner door. He tried to put her in the recovery position but she sat up. He watched her for a few seconds and decided she was safe. Then, he rose from his knees and headed clockwise to the corner. He tried to listen for sounds of entry while keeping an eye on her.

Jason heard a noise. His head turned that way. He knew his younger self was out there. He recalled the intensity of the moment but he could no longer feel it. In its place, there was nothing. His heart beat out a steady rhythm. He found it hard to appreciate that he'd have a chance to revisit this moment but here he stood. He wondered what Simon was thinking.

He turned to look back at Sally and was startled to find her standing next to him. He gazed into her unseeing eyes. He wasn't certain which way Simon would come round, but reasoned he would be drawn to her, if only for the sake of curiosity. Sally was in no shape to stop a cold. She might stop Simon by virtue of being recognisable. Jason could hear footsteps and had to move quickly. He moved around her as silently as he could and stepped into a room. Jason heard approaching footsteps. They stopped. There followed a familiar voice.

"You look like Sally but you're not her. There's no way she could have made it in to the building, ahead of me. Also, you're wearing different clothes. So, who are you?"

Jason thought he was being quiet but Simon seemed to sense him.

"Who's there?" Simon called out. "I know you're there. I can hear you breathing."

Jason didn't believe that. He often wondered how Simon would know when to stop talking because others were in earshot. Jason wasn't sure whether to stay out of sight and call his bluff, or step out and directly influence the moment. In the end, he remained concerned for Sally.

Jason stepped out from the room and into the corridor for the showdown Sally wanted but hadn't shown up for. Simon was smaller than memory served him. He knew that he'd grown up now but his friend should still be taller. Jason had even asked Santa for a growth spurt one Christmas, to catch up with him. He had wondered if Simon's dad had been a giant.

Simon took a step back. Black curly hair sat on top of a concerned face. It was a relief to see him again, standing up under his own power. So mesmerised by this moment and on the cusp of changing his situation, Jason handed the initiative to Simon.

"Who are you and what have you done with my friend?" Simon spoke first.

Jason looked at Sally. "I've done nothing to her." He looked back at Simon. "I can't let you go by, for her sake. It's the only way to save her."

Simon appeared to be weighing his options.

"I can't fight a man. You win."

Jason wasn't sure about this but Sally chose that moment to

convulse and he put his hands on her shoulders to steady her. It lasted only a moment and, when he next looked up, Simon had moved. Jason kept one hand on Sally's shoulder and turned sharply to see Simon standing next to the other corner.

"No, wait," called Jason, standing up.

"You snooze, you lose," chided Simon.

Jason needed to halt Simon's escape. Sally seemed stable now, so he moved towards him. Simon sprinted away. When he reached the door, he crashed through it. Jason reached it as it slammed shut. Through the window of the inner door, he looked ahead to see his younger self. He wished he was looking at a mirror. A face from his recent past, yet less than half his age. He'd thought he was indestructible. His younger self stared in through the outer glass door, with a face angrier than he thought possible. The hateful face was turned to its left and angled down a little. Simon had gone down the stairs. Again. History hadn't repeated itself. History was flowing the way it had before. Older Jason couldn't follow because he would lose Sally. Also, older Jason couldn't follow because younger Jason didn't see a man chase his friend down the stairs. That would have put a whole other layer of complication on the situation.

Older Jason sank to his knees, rather than risk being seen. It happened like he remembered it.

Should I come back and try again?

It didn't strike him as a good idea. Something had happened to Sally. It made no sense to linger here, in this time, unless they could make sense of it.

I made him run. Well done me. I left him no alternative.

He looked at Sally, who was motionless. *Maybe, being here, we changed the future. If we hadn't been here, would Simon have just wandered round the building, maybe laughed at me some more from inside the main door? There was no reason to take to the stairs. He was pincered by me on the inside and the outside. He had nowhere else to go.* What would have happened if Simon had gone upstairs? Something, nothing; he would never know.

Older Jason waited behind the inner door. He recalled it wouldn't be long until the small ball of anger that made up his younger self's face pulled away. The outer door did not open to an emotional fist or foot. Only later that evening would the anger flip into guilt: when Simon didn't come home, when the adults arranged the search party. No one found him in the building. They didn't give it a second thought until Simon was found, almost a week later. The guilt hadn't left him since that evening. Until the green field. Old Jason wondered if he would have to be here to help Simon leave. *How would I find him?*

He eased himself up and leaned away from the glass. Only when he was upright and balanced, did he swivel and peer through the glass. Of his younger self there was no sign. Only then did he push open the inner door and edged forwards. He looked down the stairs; Simon wasn't there. He looked outside and to the right and there, he could see younger Jason's back as he trudged towards the stile. His younger self didn't look back and memory reminded him that his embarrassment wouldn't allow him that concession. He moved back into the inner sanctum, where he saw Sally, still upright. He picked her up in both arms and walked towards the stairs. She was alive but not alert. Jason mentally tossed a coin and decided it would have to be up. They went there less often.

There was minimal, if any, forgiveness. She swore at him for letting Simon past. She shouted at him for dragging them down a flight and a half of stairs, to where they now sat.

"It was our only chance," she said. "We have to try again."

"No," Jason countered. "It won't work."

"When did you become the expert?"

She didn't stop there. She was fractious and threw just about every slur she knew at him. They ricocheted off him, not because he didn't care, but rather because he was biding his time for an opening. When the assault eased for a moment, he stepped in.

"For a moment, the three of us stood so close, we could almost touch each other. Tell me what Simon said."

Another volley of abuse.

"All right, let's try another angle. Who picked up the newspaper from the bin?"

"It was me and I told you what the date was."

"You didn't tell me at all. I had to come out to see it for myself. So, what happened next?"

"Did you remember having a drink? When did I pick you up?"

She challenged him that it was all some kind of game. A trick being played on her. She said he was laughing at her behind his serious face, but he didn't say anything. She said he had carried her, just now. She looked calmer and Jason sensed the moment had arrived to explain his theory. It pretty much boiled down to: you can't be in two places at once. He thought that he could because his body had changed. But, if they were both to go back to that time, they'd both be in trouble. Maybe more for her because she'd be in the area three times. He wasn't going to risk it. This was the truth. This was their reality and they were stuck with the choices they had made. It wasn't fair but there was nothing that could be done.

♙♟♙♙♙♙♙

Sally was unhappy. She wanted to blame someone or something, but there were no easy candidates. They could go down to the bottom floor again. To confront the pair that ran the place. The only way to do that, if she understood it all, would be to arrive right at the death, so there would be no repercussions. Only, they'd just left there. And, if Jason was right, they couldn't go back. If he wasn't right, what could they do? Sally pretty much told them to watch their backs. No amount of diplomacy would fix that.

It wasn't fair. They couldn't go back but how could they live, knowing what they knew? Seeing what they'd seen? If no force on this Earth could stop it, then what was the point of continuing? He was implacable. When he'd come back from the first flight, he'd changed. Not just on the outside but inside too. He left a part of himself back there, somewhere in space. The young Jason had grown up so fast, there wasn't the space for him in the old one.

It was hard to look at him. No matter how she did it, she still couldn't picture the puzzled young boy who lived next door. This man wouldn't tap on the wall in the night to let her know someone was there. To let her know she wasn't alone. She looked at his face. She knew well enough that a surface of calm could hide a deep sea of turmoil. She felt guilty for thinking of this in her own terms. Maybe all this stoicism was his way of coping. Maybe the body was protecting itself. His subconscious must have boxed up all his fears, terrors and emotions somewhere safe, then hung up the key. She reached out to him and gave him a hug. It was a moment before she felt his arms around her shoulders. She was upset. She was upset for him because he could not be upset for himself. She caught herself mid-sob and the emotion flipped on its head. She raged at the unfairness of it. He'd been taken away from her and she'd been taken away from him. What was left of Jason was nothing short of an injustice. She was angry and she needed someone or something to blame. She knew exactly the target.

"Follow me," she ordered.

Jason nodded at her as they went upstairs, then down. There

were no masks today. No changing colours. No slick clouds of smog sucked into the foyer. They stopped one floor below. The landing should have been raging back at them but it was subdued. It wasn't placid but it certainly wasn't shooting out bolts of lightning.

The next flight down were the guards. They might be there. Might. Maybe. Outside, lengthening shadows reached away towards the hill. The sun was very low on the other side of the building. Sally asked Jason how long it had taken her to lose her marbles. It hadn't been long before she started to drift away.

"We might just have time, then," she mused. She felt her eyes glowing as she spoke.

It's time to finish this. Cut the head off the snake.

She looked into Jason's eyes. On another day, on another face, they were the eyes set in a face of stone. Today they were in the face of a friend who had suffered so much. She smiled. She had the answer.

"Let's go," she said and turned away. She managed no more than one step before she was brought up short.

"Not this time."

She turned, looking questioningly at Jason.

He reminded her of the last idea she'd had to solve their problems. The plan had been to stop Simon but all they had achieved was to ensure it happened. How could they know that what would happen here would prevent anything? It could make it worse. She needed to explain what she wanted and how it was going to work. Her eyes dropped to Jason's chest and the wall, before coming to a rest on the stairs. He was right. She couldn't bear to look up straight away, in case he looked back. Her voice joined in for the ride, but confidence was somewhere between there and the stairs.

She explained it all. The source. The heart of the problem.

They were here to attack it at the earliest opportunity, which fortunately meant they wouldn't bump into themselves. One last time. One last opportunity. The clean corridors lit themselves, but in a subdued manner.

Just outside the toilets, Jason put a stop to proceedings.

"I need something to eat and drink. Probably a lot of both and maybe some to keep, for later. A shower would be good, too."

She felt a pressure to push on and do this now in case the moment was lost. Even in a place where moments were endless, there were precious few available. She agreed it had been a long time since they had eaten, although she hadn't fully noticed it until he'd mentioned it. She delayed it a little while, when she declared she was going to have to wash, first. It was the first thing she'd looked forward to, in a while. Jason went into the Gents at the same time.

Jason had ordered himself a large portion of what he used to call boring vegetables and some boiled chicken. Something healthy, in case he didn't get to eat properly for a while. It wasn't what a condemned man might have chosen. When Sally returned from a satisfying cleanse, he was halfway through a meal fit for three kings. According to his own words, loving every bite.

There's no better sauce than hunger.

Next to the food was half a jug of water but no glass. It irked her that he had taken the healthy choice. She was sure he suppressed a burp while she was making her choice. She went for a large, thick pizza with a pot of tomato sauce. She often craved it and was ever disgruntled that her dad had twice as much as she was allowed. If she couldn't finish this lot, she was sure that Jason would help out.

"I'm sure your stomach is pleased by all the attention you give it," she said.

Next to his plate were two blocks that could have been

mahogany-coloured soap. When she pointed at them, he advised they were a long-term food bar. Apparently, each one allowed enough nutrients for a week. She wasn't sure if he had to peel something away, first.

"Watch this," Jason said.

He stood up and, with a finger, drew a short line on his hip. He picked up one of the bars. Moving it to his hip, the line was a pocket. It appeared out of the material and he pushed in one bar, then the other. The pocket sealed itself up when he drew his finger along the same line.

"Useful, wouldn't you agree?"

She stared, wondering why he hadn't said something to the tune of, 'How cool is that?' then reminded herself why.

"Any other discoveries?" Sally asked.

Jason's eyes narrowed, suddenly. He believed there were other people on this floor. He hadn't seen anyone but he felt sure the noises he'd heard over his eating suggested some activity around the corner.

It wasn't long before both were full of food and water. They stood up, feeling less nimble but more satisfied. They set off, with Sally in front and right and with Jason hugging the left wall. They scanned the rooms on opposite sides. A perfunctory thumbs-up from one to the other was enough to continue past each doorway. Halfway down the short length, Sally stopped as a touch of fresh air caught her senses. It could be an air conditioner but it was crisper and fresher than that. Had a door been opened, ahead or behind? Her bold advance ground to a halt. She felt tempted to retreat to the corner, just to check for any movement. If someone had come in through the main door, how much time would they have? It wouldn't take long before they raised the alarm. Each second, she expected someone to appear. Forward or back? She was caught in between. Her attention was drawn upwards, to the points of light in the ceiling. They were the smallest of pinpricks and few of them on this stretch. Half a dozen produced a light that drenched the corridor completely. Was it sunlight piped in? Was the fresh air pumped in as well?

She closed her eyes, breathed in through her nose and released the air, slowly out of her mouth. The light above her flickered and she felt the same air descending through her from top to toe. It was just the right amount of soothing and her mind allowed itself to drift away. A hand on her shoulder brought her back to the present. Jason's questioning face received a smile and a nod. It was followed up by a quizzical head tilt and a response of raised eyebrows and some gentle shooing. As she looked around, there were a few moments where everything she looked at had a blue tinge. One last glance upwards. She might not have another chance to feel the warmth of the light and the taste of the air.

As she set off again, she reflected on their first circuit of this troubled place. They were playing at secret agents. They'd leapt in and out of rooms they knew full well were empty.

Have we ever been truly alone, in here?

The herdsman who projected himself across the galaxy seemed to have been everywhere and every-when.

Sally turned the final corner and came up against the tinted door and froze. She looked up. She didn't know how much time passed, until the familiar presence joined her. Instead of the hand on her shoulder there was a gentle touch on her arm. She didn't look up. She was transfixed. There was nothing in front of her except for a tinted door and a shadowy doubt about what lay beyond. The fingers on her shoulder moved. She didn't know whether that was good or bad. She became aware of the shape of Jason overtaking her on the left as he headed towards the door. He stopped for a moment.

Is he having second thoughts too?

CHAPTER 13

Jason let his hands fall on his hips. Unconsciously, he began to mark out the shapes beneath the material. He drew a line with a forefinger and a pocket opened up. A gloved hand reached in to collect the energy bar he'd stored on that side. It had accrued no fluff or dust. It offered no smell when he brought it to his nose. Upon running his tongue along the end, he tasted fruit.

It hadn't come with any instructions. He sucked at it for a minute and wondered if that was doing him any good. Without the ability to bite off a chunk, would it satisfy his stomach? Would it reduce in size, as an ice cream might with persistent attention? Would it remain the same size until it ran out of energy, like a battery?

Jason pushed the door. It didn't open but it wouldn't have responded to that action for a millennium, or more. He double-tapped it with a finger and the panes slid apart. Ahead of them, the room was quiet. There were flat screens positioned on the wall and smaller ones on the tables. He shuffled forward, peering left and right. When he was sure the room was empty, he turned to face Sally and gave her a thumbs up. Only when Jason walked in did Sally release herself from her self-imposed stocks. She moved uncertainly. By the time she caught up, she was walking in the fashion of someone balancing books on their head.

All windows, apart from the one next to the ball showed a blue sky and sunny day. The one next to the ball was black. The sun had set before they'd eaten and night had fallen. The sun effects on the window could have been disorientating if you were unaware of the time.

The six benches were still in place a few yards from the ball, which was probably the focus of every piece of equipment in the room. Through the windows, a crescent moon hung in the night sky. The room was different. It took a while to appreciate how much. All the tables, although in the same place, had pads and pens on them. Some of the pads had been used; some of the tables, too. Jason moved his hand over one of them and parts lit up. Some showed calculations and formulae. Others had random scribbles or pictures of families. No, not pictures – here, there was movement.

A scene was revealed of a family out for a walk. At first, the camera appeared to be held by someone. The view swept up and down to the other side of the adults and children in an ellipse. The view faded and returned to the beginning. Jason moved his hand away and the image switched off.

Pens were strewn about. Small, stubby pens in two colours. Each had a tip of white, with the rest of the pen being either black or blue. He picked up one and examined it. There were two buttons, one at each end. Pressing at the blue end wrote in that colour on any surface. Pressing white erased it. Writing appeared on almost any surface regardless of the distance. The exception was the ball, which couldn't be marked.

Despite the scattered objects on desk and floor, he remembered the dangers of being too close. He looked back at Sally. She had been adamant about being here because there was something she had to do. She was unlikely to hold a grudge but he was going to need her assistance in the coming days, if he was going to be able to survive at home. He wasn't sure what future was available. Would one be chosen for him? The least likely option was to head downstairs and offer himself up as a contract pilot. He had skills that could be made use of. But didn't they have thousands of pilots? Would a life on *New Earth* appeal to him? Would they want him?

Sally was figuring out what she should do. It was the green zone again. All the build-up and then, come the moment, fear in the face of the foe.

Emotions, Jason reflected, *you could keep them.*

Occasionally, a creak drew his attention. It took a few interruptions to track it down. It came as a surprise to find it was the sphere. Here, the ball was attached to the heavy frame, fixed to the ceiling. It was hard to see it as the threat it had been before. Something rattled on the floor, which turned his head. Sally had picked up some small items from the benches and had cast them under the ball. They were passing through the zone that would have been drawn upwards on their last visit. Concerned about the noise attracting attention, he grabbed her wrist, just as she was about to hurl something else. He didn't bother removing whatever was in her fingers. He let her pull her hand free.

Sally's experiment, if you could call it that, encouraged him enough to move closer to the ball. Curiosity lured him back to the spot where, but for Sally's intervention, he would have met his end. He felt confident the pull wasn't in effect and passed the inside line of the benches. As before, he lifted an arm up as if to touch it. There was a gentle pull but nothing from which he couldn't walk away.

He turned to see if Sally had had an epiphany. Sally stood with her back to him, halfway to the door, scratching both arms at the same time. He walked up to her and put a hand on her shoulder. He didn't know what words would release her from whatever she was feeling. Any words might set something off, so best to provide a bit of comfort.

He cared. But that was about it. The feelings were restricted to that much.

Maybe that's another reason I can't go home. I don't want to. I can be anywhere. But then, if I was the boy and not the man but still without emotions, would I think this way? Or, is it that I have no choice?

Sally flitted between furtive and frantic. She demanded answers but didn't know a single question. She had always prided herself on being smarter than the average Clare. Jason suspected she might be frustrated. She, too, was out of options. She moved from her spot, initially towards him and the door in defeat, then back in defiance. He weighed up the situation.

"Maybe we should just go."

With little time left on the clock, the demons within were released at the uncaring, stoic ball. All the words that had been building up were released from behind the dam. This racket would be hard to overlook.

"You arsehole! You made this whole damn case of rubbish that it is!"

No one would accept this as environmental noise. Jason glanced across to the doors and his shoulders eased when the outburst was as short as it was heated. He took another couple of steps to encourage her into his wake. She half turned. In that split-second, time slowed for him as he saw the dying embers in her eyes light up. She picked up a heavy-looking pad from a table and poured all her anger into one last throw of the dice. Her hip snapped forward and propelled it with more pace. There was a definite crunch when it fractured on impact with the surface. The ball was solid. Jason's eyes were keen, as his face registered the closest image to surprise. He couldn't see her face but her mouth was covered by both hands.

The pad made no dent; neither did it move the ball but simply glanced away before noisily hitting the wall then falling to the floor. The ball, while heavy and seemingly unmovable, was not insensitive. Outside the building, shockwaves rippled out from the ball. The invisible effects passed away into the night. They continued through buildings, in a nearby town on an otherwise quiet evening.

In the room, the energy released from the ball overloaded the scanners, which then flat lined. It rippled through Jason's body. Sally returned towards the door, with him in pursuit. Jason was aware that trouble could pour through the doors at any minute, unless this was fixed. His attention was drawn to the window where light brightened behind the tree line as flames took hold.

It's happening again. I need to stop this. But how?

He reached out to the ball in spite of the threat. He saw it more as an energy in need of calming and not the thing it was. His hand touched the surface. The energy that had, moments ago, reverberated round his body now multiplied exponentially. He felt dizzy, tired, energised, old and young, all at the same time. The energy remained trapped inside him. The surface burned but he couldn't tell if it was hot or cold. As he withdrew his hand, there was moisture where he'd touched it.

A voice from his right rang out with the words, "What in blazing carnation are you doing? This is a restricted area. How did you gain access?"

Jason turned his head to view a tall man with a noticeable paunch. Lines around the man's eyes suggested his best years were behind him. In between challenging him and Sally, the man unconsciously tugged at the sleeves and shoulders of his lab coat. He advanced on Jason. When he'd halved the distance, Jason calmly observed his attempt to alter the balance of power. Was he the guard dog, trained to bark loudly? The tall man stuttered to a stop. Not a guard, then. He was one of those yapping dogs that barked at strangers, only when safely behind their gates.

Jason saw no stress although, if more people were alerted by the dog, the situation could become difficult. Sally wasn't in the room but she was visible through the tint. She was out of the immediate hotspot, though there was no guarantee of safety. Which was should he escape? Should he escape? If this man pursued Jason, there was a chance Sally could escape the other way. Halfway through his tactical review, his train of thought was derailed by the dampness on his fingers. For a second, his eyes went blank as he considered whether this was the forerunner to the return of fear. Wasn't it sweaty palms? Was he going to be overwhelmed by emotions about his new existence? He wished for this not to be. He'd seen what emotions were doing to Sally. He remembered what they'd done to him.

Jason rubbed his thumb along the tips of the fingers of the hand that touched the ball. Looking back at it, the ball was no longer attached to the ceiling. Their plan had failed. Again. The time to back away was now.

"Yes," the man exulted, "keep away from what you can't possibly understand."

Another change of position. Jason stopped halfway to the inner wall. The man guarded the ball from further unsolicited contact by standing between two tables. He had wedged a screen under his left bicep, secured by the vice-like grip of his left hand. In his right hand, he wielded a short, thin tube. It could have been a pen. He waved it at the ball then used it to prod the pad.

"I don't know what you've done, or how. But you've blown all the sensors in the room. I'll need to recalibrate the few that work."

"Stay away from it," advised Jason.

The man's gaze shifted from ball, to pad, to probe as he prodded and pointed. High and low tides of energy fluctuated in Jason's body. Waves came and went, increasing in power, each time.

"That's what I said to you. You're in big trouble."

As the technician turned his attention back to the ball, Jason decided it was a sensible time to depart. The man sneered.

"Think you can just walk away, without me noticing? One touch on this pad and I can lock all the doors in this place. You're mine."

His grip shifted on the probe. He lost his grip on it but it didn't fall. When he turned to catch it, it was gone. Jason's looked on. He'd warned the man already. Best to do nothing.

He noticed a name badge attached to the man's belt: Dr Gardiner. He hadn't spotted it before and only saw it now because the coat that hung to his thighs was being drawn up, towards the ball. The doctor's tie also began to curl up. Other smaller, lighter items from the tables rolled towards the window and fell upwards, disappearing into it. Then, the ball's attention turned to other nearby items. It began its assault on metallic objects. Dr Gardiner looked from Jason to the ball and back again. He turned the pad in his hand and pointed it at the ball. He tapped an ear with his free hand. It sounded like he was trying to speak with a colleague but there was a problem. His body was pulled sideways. In the instance of losing his balance, the device in his hand was jerked free and followed the other items. The man tried to back away, but he couldn't move and every attempt caused him to slide. He tapped near his ear more frantically as he was drawn closer.

"What is happening? What have you done?"

Jason could feel the pull of it from where he stood. He backed away while he could. Dr Gardiner grabbed the leg of a table. He screamed, begging Jason to go for help.

"Please," he repeated.

He tried to gasp air into his lungs. He wasn't a weak man but the muscles in his arms and fingers couldn't hold against that energy. He flailed around for something else to hold on to. When his grip on the table failed, he landed on the ball. Again and again, he tried to jump away. Jason felt the energy within him surge.

The man's hands scrambled around his terrified face. He rifled through his pockets. He gripped his coat lining for solutions, for something. He tried to reach the top of the ball but moaned as his shoes began to melt. His screams were loud with the agony of being taken apart, as bone and flesh and blood were being absorbed. Slowly, his form was reduced. Nothing escaped. Jason heard the screams from the other side of the tinted door.

Jason had stood there impassively, throughout. His experience was that the energy swamped him in repeated powerful waves. He backed away every time he felt the ball's gravity reaching out further. He had felt the imperative to save a life but knew the power of the device would only drag him in, too. He'd faced death enough times. In spite of the unfolding scene, his thoughts returned to *Shark* team. He had been powerless to prevent their demise, as others had been powerless to prevent his fate. Here he was uncertain of the limits of his new-found strength but he had seen what the ball was capable of.

Silence reigned in the room. The only sounds left were cries from beyond the door. Exiting the room, he encountered a pool of regurgitated food. The fumes were strong and caught the back of his throat. He had to fight the reflex to add to it, all the way back to the main door. He pushed air slowly out through his nose and pressed his tongue to the roof of his mouth. He stopped at the box and requested another six bars. For each one, he drew a line in his suit and inserted them.

As the inner doors slid aside, Sally was standing ahead of him, looking upwards. It was good that she'd stayed. He suspected she might not hang around, which would have complicated things. Her eyes were fixed forward, body poised like a matador, as she prepared for an onslaught. Several flashes drew his attention to the stairs. The whole stairwell was thick with red and black smoke. Lightning flashed. This was going to hurt. Two storeys up and four flights of stairs of intense assault. A flash lit up his face and dared him to enter.

How desperate are you to return home, after what you have wrought? Jason asked himself, wondering if the ball had another power, sentience. Could it somehow be angry?

As he placed a foot on the first step, a jagged line of white energy bolted from the wall and struck his knee. It was more shocking than it hurt and he withdrew his leg.

"I think the key is not to mind," Sally mumbled.

It was a bold statement, given that she had not moved since he'd caught up with her. He wondered what would shake her out of her state. He wondered whether the lightshow reflected their emotions back at them. He dismissed that thought as he hadn't had any since the green zone.

I can't say I'm missing them.

He was sure even Sally couldn't generate the levels of anger the scene ahead presented. He tried another tack and spoke several phrases up the stairs.

"It wasn't our fault. It's not fair. We came here to help our friend."

He didn't know where that last one came from. Another phrase urgently wanted to be spoken.

"You didn't stop the others, did you?"

Why am I talking to the building? We tried to find Simon and failed. We tried to stop a war and failed. Each time, we were too late.

He reached for Sally's arm. When the next flash struck her, she spoke.

"It's not hurting. Why?"

"It was your discovery."

She looked nonplussed.

"At the first landing, you pushed me through. We wouldn't have made it through, unless we were connected."

It made sense, sort of. They mounted the last flight through the flashes of lightning. Jason knew they were back to square one. How long would they have to spend trying to leave at the right time? It was a little more convenient for having moved the bin, but it was still going to be a delay. They weren't blessed with choice and would have to proceed as best they could.

"Let's go find a newspaper," he said and reached out to open the door.

CHAPTER 14

As Jason's fingers made contact, the energy released into him from the ball discharged. Time paused. His view fractured into thousands of moments. He became enveloped by periods taken out of his life, from the end, all the way back to the beginning. Sally had been right next to him but now, in this space, there was only him. He was separated from the building, from time, from himself. He had no form, no body. The perspective altered based on his thought.

The views around him were short, repeated motion clips. They were layered, they were myriad and they bombarded his attention. Space for thoughts was becoming limited as the images multiplied, until only the choices remained.

As his point of view moved within the space, light danced from the views. Beyond that, there was no light. He didn't feel trapped. He sensed an exit. Was that the end of his corporeal form? Some of the final images had no colour and little light.

As well as what he knew had happened, the layers showed links to *what ifs*. What if he had taken a different direction at a point in his life? How might it all have turned out? This is where the patterns blurred, diverged and became layered. A new path broke away from the main. Most paths that broke away, never returned. A *yes* instead of a *no* or a left instead of a right created a new layer. Sometimes, the differences were so negligible as not to be different. And here, in this disconnected space, all the options were true. He felt he recognised them all.

He needed Sally. She grounded him, brought him back to the here and now. If only she were here, they could make the right choice. Where would be the best place to find her? He should start at the end. His future self would know more. He could work back from there to find her. If he could find Simon too, that would the best outcome.

He looked for the path with the highest end. Worst case? He would end up back here, wouldn't he? Or would that be it? His view angled up and he chose the last image at the top.

He blinked and found himself standing in a darkened room, gazing at the window. The Jason that had arrived faded and was replaced by the man in this time and space. There wasn't much in the way of a view. Outside, a dark, thick fog swirled and eddied under the faint orange glow of a nearby streetlamp. The room was too warm for his liking and the air was stuffy. His breath came, short and shallow. He hadn't the energy for deeper draughts. He tried to open the window but remembered it was locked. He searched for the key but unlocking achieved no more movement. A closer inspection, tricky in the gloom, revealed that all the windows had been screwed shut.

Around the world, these wretched fumes dominated the atmosphere. Gases that no industry would generate for millennia.

"We almost did it," he declared to no one. "We were but two against the world. We could have done it, only we fell short, unable to make a difference. Hindsight, like watching the replay, is always twenty-twenty. When you're inside the game, you're lucky if you can see your hand in front of your face."

There was a change in the space behind him as the door opened. When he was young, a cough used to draw attention. Nowadays, with the poor air, coughing was par for the course. In the window, he could see weak yellow light from a desk lamp down the corridor. In front of the lamp, the shape of a woman was silhouetted and she reached for something. A cord was pulled, which fired up the light. Breathing on the embers of a fire might have given as much light. The bulb and the power system were no longer at their collective best, yet the external view was replaced by his own reflection. His looks had long since faded and the skin was pulling itself down his face. His back had been bent a little, by the years.

"You can't be standing in the dark, Master Jason," piped the woman.

The bulb above was spluttering into life and she was still a walking shadow to him. She wasn't young, either. She had the look of a woman in her forties. The lack of sun paled the skin and widened the eyes; it stripped away her youthfulness and skewed her age to older than he might have imagined. She stopped for another cough. He was familiar with that sound. He reckoned he had been among the first to hear it.

"What have I told you?"

"I was—" *What was I doing?* "I wanted some fresh air," he answered.

"Hah, you'll be lucky," she almost cackled. "There's none of that, no more. Anyways, before I forget to say, it's lunchtime. Don't wait too long this time or there won't be any."

Jason eased a breath through his nose. It brought in smells of warm air and school dinners. He wanted to fling open the windows and drown out that smell with real air. That wouldn't happen again, in his lifetime.

"Outside, it's—"

Energy leeched from his body as he spoke. He felt more tired, tonight and didn't know where to go with that sentence.

What's the use?

"That's your fault, of course," replied the shadow in the window.

A cold sensation eased its way down his back and he turned, slowly, to look at her.

She added, "Your generation, at least."

There was enough light to see her thin-lipped smile before she turned away.

Wasn't that Simon's cough from all those years back?

Fighting for air through a tide of chemicals, as Mrs G failed to maintain a stoic face.

I'm sorry I didn't save you.

All the people he'd ever met would be gone now. Life expectancy was dropping. He reckoned no one was going to be as old as him until men lived on the moon; no one was going up there soon. The countries of the world were still playing the blame game. No meaningful alliance would start today.

Jason looked at her. It was hard to tell which nurse it was, in the light. Behind where she was standing sat the microphone and box. He'd used it to add to the transcript Sally had handed him, all those years ago. He'd completed it after all. He left it late but there'd always been something else to do. He'd spent too many years listening to her voiced parts. He suspected it would never be heard. In a world full of junk, who would want a piece of a failed history? Especially when that past was the cause of so much pain? As he thought of her, he said her name, almost automatically.

"Sally—" he started, but again, speaking proved too much of a challenge to continue.

He was grateful for the minimal space between the bed and the window. He didn't have far to go to lie down.

"Yes?" replied the woman. More patience radiated from her voice this time. "Your daughter? We're sorry for your loss. Parents shouldn't have to bury their children but that's the way of things now, I suppose. She was a lovely girl. We all miss her here."

The nurse's arms twitched a little. When the bulb above

glowed a little brighter than before, he could see her hands were fiddling with something. As she left, she absent-mindedly dropped it to the floor. He watched it fall slowly, until it reached the carpet and settled amongst similar waste. A few dark patches in the surface suggested liquids had been spilled.

My time has, at last, come to an end. The next era is underway. Is it arrogant to say that? Without me, one era comes to an end. I suppose we all wish to make an impact in the world.

He didn't want to reflect on this but he couldn't escape it. He used to walk but had to stop because it tired him out. The nurses told him they weren't going to bring him back anymore. There weren't as many spare wheelchairs as there used to be. Now, standing and talking was too challenging. He thought he could call back the nurse but his voice faltered. It lacked the power and what could she do? Give him a second life for living so long? Rebirth on the meritocracy plan. And was that life worthy of anyone to endure? Better to be reincarnated as a mole. One small cog in a machine too large to see, once you're buried inside. He had made an impact, but the outcome was irreversible.

Should I be afraid? The last unknown is almost upon me. Here, alone in this darkened room, lies the funny old man who tells anyone who will listen that he used to play outside. It is a curse to have outlived my peers. Afraid? Still not. It was more disappointment that I lived long enough to see it come true. And so soon.

As he did during such moments, he thought of the girl he once knew. Had she also been allowed to live so long? Was she alone somewhere, wondering what happened to him?

It's started. I've seen the end of this story and now, I'm seeing the beginning.

Earth's peoples will suffer a cataclysm which they will have to endure. Yet, they will overcome this and take the species to the stars. They will thrive until some political think-tank starts a war so vast that the galaxy will be forever changed. I wonder how they sold the war. Did they tell everyone that the aliens had it in for us when, all along, it was us who had it in for us?

Jason sat down on the bed. Tiredness prevailed. The muscles had reached their maximum stretch from his bones. His face was much the same. Gravity was more ruthless on the body, as the years became decades. The strength within faded and, before you knew it, you had to work hard just to stand still. Lunch was too much for him, today. It took him a good while to lie himself down. With effort, he lifted his legs from the floor and lay flat on the bed. He had to rest for a while, to recover.

He lay on his bed, noisily inhaling the warm air. The overtones of lunch weren't as strong now but dinner would be along before the aroma completely faded. Not that the food was any different. Root vegetables grown in vast greenhouses, under lighting. Maybe a little green on your potatoes, for taste. He raised his head to look around. It took more effort than it should have. First, he had to think about moving, then build up the reserves to move his muscles.

The first time I was this tired, it was due to that green field. Now there are no green fields. Wasn't it bad enough, without all this effort?

It reminded him of the storeroom that Sally had been so worked up in. Why had that thought come to him? These rooms have it all, except a bin. Opened tins of food scattered on the desk, the chair, or tossed aside onto the floor. Clothes piled over the top of them. Old boxes stacked on top of each other, or on their side. Some empty, some containing what was scribbled on the side and others containing who knew what. He had looked when he first arrived but wasn't interested now. He doubted it was important but it was being kept here, just in case. There were some shelves on the walls, but some had broken and fallen to the floor. Some boxes lay open with their contents spilled around them in the darkness.

There wasn't much to break up the darkness, which could be a blessing. A subdued glow emanated from the door to his left. Between that and the tired bulb that hung above him, there was a gesture of light. He couldn't read under it. Rain fell against the window. For a moment, he longed to be under it, one last time. It wouldn't be pleasant though. But the feel of rain, one last time? No, it wasn't worth the air.

The light from the door broadened as someone came in with another box. It was unceremoniously dumped in his room. Every other footstep crunched or cracked something. More solid things were pushed aside with the foot. No one kicked anymore. It had led to broken bones. In the dark, it was hard to see what you were kicking.

More junk, less space and soon, more smell. His breathing became noisier. His ears were overtaken by the sound. It was harder now. His lungs weren't up to the task. He thought about the past again. What else was there to think of? He knew how the future would unfold. It was best not to think about it.

I can't remember when I arrived here, but I know Sally's face like I'd seen her yesterday.

The present kicked back in, as he opened his eyes. Everywhere was full and so were the seas. All their waste was now being disposed of, if that was the right term, around them. Why have a bin when you can't take it away anyway?

He remembered Simon under that light and now, it would end with this bulb. It pulsed in time with his heart. Both, he noticed, were slowing. The cold rushed through his body. It wasn't fair.

Why does it have to end?

That was the only sensation he felt, anymore but each rush of adrenaline weakened his heart a little more.

I'm jump-starting a car at the edge of a cliff. What gives me life also takes it away.

He was alone.

Is it too much to ask for a little love?

He thought of his wife and children. He hadn't seen his grandchildren for so long. It had been hard for them to see him. They'd told him he already had great-grandchildren. What lives would they have? He wished he could feel the warmth of the sun on his face. His hands gripped the bedsheets for the minimal comfort they offered. His body went cold but he also felt the sensation of damp inside his single-piece outfit. There may have been a whimper but there wasn't anyone to hear it.

Another bulb in an unremarkable building flickered and died.

CHAPTER 15

The light in one frame flickered and faded. The light in another, twinkled and attracted his attention.

A flurry of flashes captured the moment and drew Jason into the moment. He stuffed a hand into his pocket and reminded himself of the past. There was a certain amount of comfort in feeling his old phone, even if it no longer worked. He should have handed it in for recycling, years ago. To save the planet, they'd said. The networks shut down, at any rate. He had hung onto it, hoping the ban was only temporary. It was taboo to show them in public these days. Although, what good would handing it in have done? It was said the trace materials could be recycled into other industries but it was never as easy as they said. Rumours of huge landfill sites abounded. Radio had a revival but there was talk of tearing down the transmitters. The consequence of not being able to hide in your phone was to look up but there was little to see. People returned to looking down.

The sun was locked behind a perpetual haze. Only a few years ago, it was still too bright to look at directly. It was obvious that something wasn't right. Once, such a sight spoke of humidity or pollution. So much was electric now that it had to be something else. Particulates settled in the atmosphere; some fell as rain. Breathing ailments were increasingly common.

There had just been a breeze and he let it play with his hair, rather than dare to inhale too deeply. Most people responded to the turn of events by wearing masks. A few wore swimming goggles as well. The wooden chairs around him had all emptied. The last of the crowd was moving to one of the simple brick buildings, up the slope. Around him, small rectangles and writing carved into grey stone proliferated. A solitary figure at the rear of the departing group paused, turned and headed back down the slope.

He was at another funeral. This time it was Carole's. His wife. They all seemed to blur, these days. Black was the new black. There was an almost constant state of mourning. Even under the weight of all the loss, his emotions remained locked away. Tears were a rare commodity. Perhaps, that was for the best. Too much loss can break you down.

The branches of the sycamores swayed idly in a breeze. The grass was yellowing, though there was a dampness in the air that caught in his throat. He looked at the tree again. There were fewer leaves than he expected and most of them were turning the same colour as the grass. Autumn? No, this wasn't the falling season. This was spring and grass was always green, unless there was a dry spell. And then he saw it, if only just. He saw the sun, though it was obscured by a thick fog. It was a pale silver disc behind the haze. This was the first time he had ever looked directly at the sun without it hurting his eyes.

He placed a hand against his face for a long moment, until a younger voice spoke to him.

"Are you coming, Father?"

He looked at his daughter. She'd left the group to come and rescue him from himself. She'd restrained her shoulder-length hair into a ponytail today. She looked up at him with her green eyes, set into the marble of her pale skin. Emeralds set into white gold, he had told her, from before she could walk. By the time she escaped her teens, she looked the spit of his own mother. He'd named her Sally, in memory of the one who'd got away.

"You know I'd rather you didn't call me that."

"You fathered me. I wasn't *dadded*."

"I might have sired you. Could you call me *sir* or *milord*?"

"You can only sire vampires. As I saw you checking yourself in the mirror before we came out, I'm almost sure you're not one."

"Almost?"

"I'm prepared to allow room for doubt, pending further research."

She offered a short laugh as he shook his head. Her laugh turned into a cough, which she quickly silenced. Once she started, she couldn't stop. He thought she suppressed it around him, to try and make him feel better. Even now, it must be burning in her lungs. This way must be making her worse but he allowed her the moment. When she spoke again, it was in controlled, short sentences.

"You must come. To the wake. Martin brought your grandson. To meet you."

"I've met him. You stayed over at mine, last night."

"You can take that attitude. If you want. You don't have to see him..."

Jason sighed.

"As you're twisting my arm. Again."

She turned away. He hesitated until she'd walked a couple of paces, then turned back to look at him. She'd survived into adulthood. She was the only one who had. He wondered if that was some gift from *The Project* or a bad joke, turned worse with age. She was much less well than she'd been, even last year. He had hoped she would have his healthy genes. Although he couldn't help but wonder if the onesie he'd reluctantly put on before flying into space was keeping him healthy. He had survived long enough to suffer. Only the good die young. Except they don't. He knew well enough what became of the young.

A few order of service leaflets blew around in the wind. Some were left behind. There wasn't a danger of them becoming collectibles. The number of attendees was lower than expected. They may have been at other, similar functions. Whatever was in the air had taken Carole. He felt certain of that. He recognised his wife's and his daughter's coughs from the one that had troubled Claude and Simon.

Beyond the immediacy of this situation, there were far fewer people out of doors than there used to be. With little sun and less fresh air to enjoy, most people stayed at home. Occasional walkers, fewer joggers and just the odd cyclist, most with a cloth mask over their faces, hurried by. Holiday destinations advertised clean air that only the richest could afford.

The wake was the usual affair. It was one of the few times people could gather and let down their masks. After a circuit of the room, he noticed that all of the guests were her friends. The last of his own friends had passed on, months ago. There were a couple of people he didn't recognise and he wondered if Mr Knight was checking in on him, as per his promise. Jason had started to lie about his age, lowering it, lest people call him out. No one in the room was older than him, and the few within ten years didn't look well. He was pretty much guessing his age at any rate, so a few years' difference was of no importance.

He thought of making a few more friends, when he stopped to chat to people in the street. Loneliness was on the rise, with death rates exceeding birth rates around the world. Life expectancy was shorter, it was hard on the heart to connect then lose someone. The loss of his wife surprised the family. It was true they'd known for a while, so they'd both had time to prepare. He should have felt something, though. Maybe it would come, in time.

The effort of repeatedly coughing wore out the lungs, muscles and tissues. Draw in a deeper breath to try and clear it, and the state of the air sent you back to square one. The guests had said their goodbyes and drifted away. He sought out his daughter before she left.

"Sally?"

"Right here, Father."

She looked lovely. He felt her arm thread between his elbow and body, holding his arm close to her.

"I'm sorry, Sally, it's all my fault."

"Father, we have talked about this. Stop it."

"I was thinking about your brother. He died so young. Your mother and I were inconsolable. I don't think she ever dealt with it, until you were born. Maybe not even then."

He looked up at the sky, for a moment. The sun dimmed as a thicker patch of smog passed in front of it. He looked down at his daughter and spoke clearly one last time to her.

"You are a wonderful mother."

He had wanted to say those words, long ago. She smiled and turned and hugged him. They didn't meet as often as he liked and he tried to fix her face in his mind. He wanted to capture this moment, forever. He blinked his eyelids like a camera, hoping one of the visions would be the perfect shot.

CHAPTER 16

On the other side of the window, a bird flew in front of the sun and the light falling on Jason flickered. He covered his mouth and nose with his hands, pressing his thumbs gently under his chin. He lowered his hands into a prayer pose, with the tips of the forefingers touching his lips. Though the room saw a lot of use, light here filtered through the dust that hung in the air. It smelled of old, heavy books that yellowed at the edges. It reminded him of the school library. This mustiness gave the room an aroma of something historic that he found calming. Where he sat, the smell had been overpowered by sweat. Not his. It would have come from the predecessors, in his position.

Jason was presentable, in trousers, a tie and an ironed shirt. All fashioned from the one suit he had. He stood behind a long desk. There were plenty of them, in this large room but this one was for him, alone. He knew that, but not because he'd been well briefed. He'd been here before. The main desk, that is the one at the far wall, was where the decision was going to be made. Again. Behind it sat the magistrates. Considering the experiences he had before, he would be lucky to walk away again. *Where was Sally when he needed her?* He could do with her being near. His shoulders sagged knowing that ship had sailed.

Two of the magistrates were new. The third, the one who sat in the middle, had whispered in turn to the others as Jason had entered. Between those three and him were the lawyers and the clerk. The lawyers didn't have a lot of desk space but they made the most of it with their books. A few loose documents were waved or leafed through to emphasise a point. Today, the witness area, to the left, was empty. It wasn't that there weren't any. It was that they had already spoken. It was the same old stuff, in the same old order, with the same old question: why were they still having to come here?

He couldn't believe he'd been caught, this time. He'd done his homework and staked the place out, every afternoon for a month. What few staff there were on a Saturday were all leaving when he walked to the main door. Prior to striding across the car park, he had changed his outfit, to give the appearance of a cleaner. He reached the door armed with a red bucket with some cleaning items, plus a rag. He'd even held the door open for the last of the leavers, with his head bowed to make the show of deferment to them. Once inside, he took nothing for granted. He'd put on a show of cleaning for an hour. This ensured any late departures were flushed out, before he made his move. He'd navigated round to the large office and spotted the space where a desk could easily have been placed. He'd paused at the edge of the space, where he imagined the benches would be placed, in the future. If he'd raised a hand, would it feel damp from the ball? Even millennia before its creation, it was imposing itself on the room.

He had brushed his fingers on the windowsill. He liked to think that there was a sparkle that infused his body and gave him access to secret places. He had turned back the way he'd come and it all went black. When he woke up, he was outside. Two paramedics were kneeling beside him and looking down with concern. Jason had seen the electric paddles next to his body and the torn shirt. Behind the medics was a police officer. Jason had groaned, inwardly. The tending medic had said his body behaved as though it had received an electrical shock. What the medic couldn't establish was that there had been no visible entry point. Without that, the conclusion was that he should stay at the hospital overnight, for tests. When he was finally discharged by the ward, he was arrested. They'd charged him yards from the corridor, where he'd sat waiting for Mrs G. Somewhere in that office had to have been a trap or a weapon. He hadn't noticed it before, and it started him thinking about where it might be positioned. It was a battle of attrition, of wills. He would win in the end.

He had shouted the last time he was here.

"You don't understand, I need to go back there. They took something from me." It was more for emphasis than stress.

The magistrate had said, "Mr Summer, if you do not restrain yourself, I will refer this case to the County Court, who may well impose a custodial sentence. You have been tried for several counts of trespassing on the same premises, in addition to applying for work therein. My advice to you is that you let go of whatever compulsion is drawing you to that building. One more visit to my chambers from you will result in significantly less leniency. Do you understand?"

On this occasion, the magistrate declared, "It is fortunate, from a punishment perspective, that you collapsed outside the building. If you had entered again, I would not have hesitated in a firmer conclusion. There is a duty of care that needs to be considered. Your case will be referred to the Health Department for a six-month period, while they monitor your condition. If you can find it within yourself to remain healthy and free of fresh charges, there will be no need for us to discuss matters again."

Outside? But I'd made it in. I know I did. I stood in the shadow of the ball and touched the window.

The magistrate carried on.

"To summarise, *if* you transgress and trespass on their property again, there *will* be a referral. Regardless of your health, there shall be an escalation. I will see to it, personally. I highly recommend you turn your attention to a more profitable endeavour. This is not a conversation. Do not misinterpret my tone. You are to leave this place and not return."

The verdict was much the same as it was, then. Before, he'd put on the apologetic face and voice and had escaped a more serious sanction. This time, he simply looked lost. Jason stood quietly behind his bench, his knuckles whitened by the intensity of his grip on the desk. A few breaths and he hung his head.

"That will be all."

A number of people filed out, mingled in the corridor for a few minutes of discussion, then headed off to other tasks. Jason watched as another group went in. Jason sat on his own. One of the court officials had tersely handed him a telephone number. It had a name preceded by 'Dr' and he was told to call it by the end of the day. Sunlight streamed in through the window. The feel of its touch on his face gave him a moment of hope.

So lost was he in what had been said, he didn't realise someone was there. His eyes scanned upwards from the polished black shoes, to the pinstriped trousers and the matching waistcoat, over a white shirt and tie. Between the tie knot and receding forehead was a clean-shaven face. It was Jason's legal representative. He was reading through some papers in a folder, with occasional bursts of furious scribbling. For several minutes, he didn't acknowledge Jason. More time passed. Jason clutched his scrap of paper, while the suited man stood with a sheaf of legal documents. Jason decided to make the call now, while the lawyer was finalising his notes but, as he stood up, the scribbling man spoke.

"I won't be a moment."

But he was – or, at least, he was much longer than what Jason thought a moment should be. He tried again.

"I'm going to make a call from the reception. When you're

done, we can talk. Assuming there is no other action I need to take."

The man stopped writing and managed to look offended.

"What's the hurry? For someone with no appreciation for process, you are an impatient one, aren't you?"

Jason explained he had to make a call. There was little to be gained from arguing and he wasn't interested in the other man's concept of time.

"As you wish. My summary of your situation is the same as last time. Nice work, in there. I'll eat tonight and a few more nights hereafter. At some point, you'll go to gaol and I'll work on your appeal, in between lunches with the company. All good stuff, when dealing with repeat offenders."

"Not exactly the post-match analysis I was hoping for."

The other man smiled, turned and walked away. After a few paces, he stopped, turned back. He held up a hand and wiggled a wrist, showing off an expensive-looking watch.

As Jason's eyes were drawn to the timepiece, the man's face melted. No, it blurred as he morphed. He became older. The watch on his wrist changed from a dark brown, leather strap to a reflective, grey metallic bracelet. Jason was mesmerised by the form, changing before him. His eyes couldn't turn away. Even the man's shoes changed. Nausea rose and fell. Barely a second after it started, it ended. The main retained his waistcoat and gained a silver streak in his hair. Jason recognised him as the holographic man who claimed to be on another planet. Sally had called him Knight.

"How did you—"

"Genetic manipulation, distortion of energy fields or magic. Pick one, or more. It all amounts to camouflage. Magic is probably your best shot. Perhaps not the genetic manipulation, as changing my genes won't change my jeans. Maybe that's why it's more than one, or maybe none of the above. Who knows? Certainly not you and I'm not willing to say."

An overconfident smile stretched from ear to ear and, with another client, could have concluded with emergency dental work. Jason was certainly concerned with the turn of events, but he wasn't on the path to anger.

"No, I really meant it," continued Knight. "I look forward to seeing you again and again here. You never give up, do you? The thing is – the important thing – is, you're a dedicated and logical individual. If only you could apply this attitude to work and not working out how to break in."

Jason had tried to work out where he had gone wrong, last time. He had sought employment in the building. He had acquired night-sight technology, albeit limited to his finances, and watched the building. Despite this, he had still been caught as soon as he'd stepped inside.

The man continued, "Oh, with this system I can be anyone, anywhere."

He changed again. It was much quicker, this time. His body shrank and he changed into Sally. Not the last time Jason had seen her but the way he remembered her. Young, when they had been a trio, before the building. Seeing her again, even like this, was grounding. It wasn't her but it was as a good an image of her, as he would ever see.

"An image taken from your memory of her. Maybe it is genetic, after all."

Something was on his mind.

"Why was I found outside, this time?"

The image of Sally regarded him for a few seconds.

"We had a project that required adjustment. The police would have been an inconvenience. They are unable to resist the itch of the building, given past. That's why they're so keen to talk to you each time and secure your release. The magistrates, though, have had enough. *I'll wait for you, Jason.*"

Jason's disinterested response may have been hard to understand, for most. Instead, he resorted to adding doubts in his own voice.

"Did she say that to you, or was it me?" taunted the man.

Jason closed his eyes. After a prolonged silence he opened them again to find the image of the man in front of him.

"Remember, boy, I can be anyone, anywhere, anytime. I'm your worst undercover copper or," he smiled again, "your best. Why do you think our time has so little crime?"

Jason thought, but didn't say, that no crime could compare to the murder of the planet. He did say, "And how many died in your war?"

"My war? My dear boy. It was you who opened the door for us."

"That old chestnut again. It didn't mean you had to come through. You could have closed it. Instead, you burned it all down. You're no better than poison ivy. Using something great to climb to the top, while killing what you're scaling."

The lawyer responded with a single clap.

"Very good, Mr Sumner – or, is it Summer now? Did your young friend tell you that? Not a very creative name change, but it works."

In two heartbeats he changed to the last vision of Sally that Jason had seen. When he'd stayed over. Then, he quickly changed to the younger version.

"How do you do that? Are you human or the product of some genetic, freak lab experiment?"

The man smiled. "Now, now, Mr Summer. I don't think your young friend told you that. It's too crass for her. She's a lovely girl, you know. Lovely skin."

There was no anger. No irritation. However, Jason decided the man had pushed a bit too far. He grabbed the man's collar and tie knot in one hand.

"I'm surprised you're not in hospital more often. Sally was right. You won't last long on *New Earth*."

The man was equally calm.

"Assault, too, Mr Summer?" He laughed, as though nothing could hurt him. "I can recommend a good lawyer."

Jason released his grip and the man's tie eased out through his fingers. He turned his back on the shapeshifter and thought about the next way in to the building.

"Maybe I was her all along. Maybe she never existed. Your whole life could be a complete lie. I will, however, offer you some small respite. Something I think you have overlooked. You do know that no one works in there, don't you?"

Jason turned to face the man.

"Then who were all those people? I watched them coming and going."

"And you did it so diligently. We were watching you too, in the warm and the dry. The people are holograms, so not really people, at all. They pull up in their cars, which are also holograms, and drive away. When they go down empty roads, or when no one is paying them any attention, they fade away. Similarly, they appear in the mornings, literally out of thin air and head to work. Some arrive early, some later, some need to head out in the morning. The random activity hides a lot of other movement by actual people in and out of the premises. I don't know why I'm telling you this. Maybe I want to see the look on your face as you try to figure out what is true. Realistically though, what are the chances of someone touching that window, then seeing stairs that hadn't been there, before? They would be sure to take a look. You did. It's simply too risky to have actual people in there, from this time.

"I look forward to seeing you again. Perhaps next time, we can look up some community service for you. You do a reasonable job of cleaning. You can start by moving the bin back to where it should be."

Jason had tried to redress the pain they had suffered by going back in there and correcting his mistakes. He'd wanted to exonerate them. Until now. Until he heard Sally's voice again. Even through the filter of Knight's control. Somehow, it cut through all the choices, good and bad, the threats and the lies.

Long term, he knew what was coming and he couldn't resign himself to that future. Unless there was no other choice. He stood at the crossroads. He was empty without her, and missing Simon, too. He needed their advice. Maybe he should have gone with her, wherever she went. There was nothing for either of them here.

It was decision time. Go back and try it, one more time? Dare to face the court one more time or put it all behind him for a new path?

As the man walked away from him and left the building, sunlight flickered through the revolving doors in front of the reception.

CHAPTER 17

"I'll wait for you, Jason," was the last thing Sally said to him in earshot.

He'd looked into her sweet, sparkling eyes and wondered who would return. She'd smiled at him, reached up and patted his cheek and told him it would be all right. She had stepped to the door, pushed it open, revealing the police tape they had ignored when they arrived, earlier that day. She looked back for a long time and radiated a warmth he could never share, then ran off into her life.

At the start, she'd ducked under and around the scaffolding, run to the edge of the big red hut, turned and waved. She turned every ten paces to wave. It was lovely to watch her smile and run and then turn back again. Jason, meanwhile, had to adjust his position to see past the scaffolding poles. He held onto the open door and kept a foot planted inside. As she neared the hedge, she stopped waving and walked backwards, until she was at the last point that they could see each other. She stood there for a long time. Initially, he thought she was looking at him. She could have been taking it all in. Him, the building, the past and the future. She might have been crying. Jason checked his watch as subtly as he could. She had stood there for at least half an hour. She was in the pose of someone in between two states. Between moving on and running back.

Truth be told, he didn't want her to go. There had been other suggestions. Other times to which the building had access. It had to be this way. Any change of location or time, and they'd both have to learn how to fit in. This choice wasn't ideal. It was a best fit. She would return to the life they'd had. Without him. Without Simon.

Jason had stood in the toilets, looked in the mirror and wondered just how old he was. With Sally beside him, they'd estimated his appearance as somewhere in the late twenties. It could be higher or lower but that seemed a safe bet. How long would she have to grow before they would reunite? Twelve years was the figure they had agreed on.

She waved and turned away. He waved back but didn't move for a while, in case she returned. She told him that she would wait. But that was now. A lot could happen, in between. Somewhere out of sight, she was probably talking to his dad, trying to explain that Jason had gone missing. She'd searched for hours, all to no avail. They'd gone to find out what happened to Simon. Yes, the police had told them not to go but they had gone anyway. Simon was important to them. Just as they were about to come home, Jason had found a way in. She'd waited for him. And waited. She hadn't wanted to leave in case he was in trouble. It wasn't much of a story but, so soon after Simon had been left in his state, they hoped it would carry enough weight. Over-embellishing a tale made it easier to drive in a wedge. She needed to stick closer to the truth. It made it easier, when memory let you down. She could say she'd seen him go in the building but had never seen him leave. She would have to omit the part that she'd seen him as she left. The act of hiding a truth within a lie. In time, she could say feelings were the reason for not being completely honest, as her parents wouldn't agree. His father would work on the solution, because that was his way.

Jason wondered if she was watching him through the hedge or if she was already knocking on his front door.

What's Dad going to think?

His body wanted to go through the motions of despair and crumple to the floor but his mind refused to play along. It was all gone. All of it. No home, no family. Nothing. He had nothing and he felt nothing.

Now she was gone. He waited. They'd agreed she should go to his dad, first. If he wasn't in, she should come back. Explaining the story to her parents first would not be a good idea. She'd stood there for half an hour. She wasn't coming back now. He stepped in, closed the door and locked it. He recognised that a number of options had been taken from him forever. Likewise, if he went down or up. There was still a chance for him to run after her. To find a way, somehow, but that wasn't part of the plan she'd made him agree to. A lethargy overtook him and he slouched to wall and floor. He could sit here for as long as he wanted.

In the absence of his feelings, it wasn't love that would have propelled him from the door, it was his lost youth. The unknown impact it would have on his life. He was a casualty and, though his dad had not been involved, Jason had been orphaned by events. This was the hard part. He knew it but he didn't feel it. Just before they saw the dinosaur, he wanted to go home but they were distracted. Before he knew it, there was a war and it had all gone wrong.

I bet they knew. I bet that man and the Computer woman knew.

They certainly didn't seem surprised when he returned. She'd laughed.

If only I hadn't done that. If only I hadn't done that one thing and then another and another. If only. Except for this meaningless building, I have no place to go. The only thing I have left now is Sally and, by the time I see her again, she will have changed.

Who would come back to meet him? It would be her but how different would she look? How different would she be inside? His ageing had taken seconds and he was back with her in an hour. Her ageing will happen in real time but he would see her in about an hour.

He'd told her it might feel like an interrogation that never goes away. The questions will never let up. Sentences will repeat: 'Now tell us the truth' or, 'What really happened, out there?' until they ring in your ears. People at school would ask her, too. Without a body, there is only the witness. During the time when Simon was missing, the police kept coming back with the same questions. Jason wondered if they were after one moment, one small mistake where he would forget himself.

Her parents might try and move away but the story would follow her. All the people there would at least know her from before these incidents. Any new town and it would be all they'd talk about. There would be no repeat of last time. No sick person would emerge from the building. There would be a child who never came home.

He thought about his dad. The man had lost his wife and now their only child. That part of his life was gone. Then he thought about his friend, lying in that bed, and imagined what life he would have. It would be the cruellest of outcomes if his friend recovered and all of this had been for nothing.

But that couldn't happen, could it? He didn't wish his friend ill but, thinking back to the hospital bed, he couldn't become much more unwell. What if both of them grew up without him? Some hearts can be true. Some can change. All he had to look forward to was seeing Sally again and trying to make a life with her.

He sat on the floor and looked out through glass, scaffolding and tape. He realised he couldn't sit here for long after all. His dad would likely come here and check out the place and try his luck on the windows. He should move downstairs and watch for the signs but the seconds ticked by. He made sure the door was locked.

He looked down the stairs, expecting a horror show but it was blank. He didn't even feel any pins and needles. Was he old news to the building now? Not worth its effort to fight against? He went down to the fifth step. The dark red fog had waited for him but there was nothing else, there. No sparks or flashes of lightning. He looked at the tree where the bin once was and waited.

The streaks appeared on the tree in regular order. Four yellow and a fifth in white. Had she run out of yellow or decided upon a different colour, to mark the milestone? Was it a white flag in paint form and she was giving up? Was she all right? He wouldn't be able to ask her for a few more years – or minutes. What if she didn't paint again? He could use the newspapers but that was slow. He almost smiled at himself. Slow compared to what? A year passed by every minute. What exactly was slow?

A sixth line appeared. Yellow again. Then all the stripes disappeared. He breathed out when seven appeared at once. Had she moved away? Had someone caught her? He thought the eighth was late. Number nine, too.

The tenth was in yellow. No special colour for this milestone. Maybe number five was a one-off. He returned to the floor once late at night and moved the bin to foyer, between the flights of stairs. On his way back to the door, he pulled out the discarded newspaper. The headlines were broadly the same, with different names, and there was nothing in there that drew his interest. The date confirmed what the tree had told him. Inasmuch as the new location for the outdoor bin was accepted, the patrons of the building accepted this one, too. With Jason sitting on stairs that were non-existent, at least to them, he could look or reach up and check the date, without going far.

Eleven, then the fine-tuning. He assumed she wouldn't paint a stripe on his twelfth birthday since they parted. By the time he saw it, months would pass before he could exit the building. Jason didn't notice anyone around, inside or out. Was it a weekend again?

Up and down. Down and up. Hours of this. He was aware of the time passing but what did that mean here? After six hours work, all he had to show for himself was being two days short. He edged down then leaned until he saw the shadow bend, extend, then broaden as night fell. Sun up, over and down. Sun up, over and stop. Stop. Back up. Now what? Today was the day. It had all come down to this. This moment. His eyes were drawn to movement along the original line of the footpath. It was a woman. It could be someone he knew. Best to go and check the time and maybe a little more. He wedged today's newspapers into the door frame. He made absolutely sure the door wouldn't close while not looking too open either and walked over.

They would meet at the tree. Halfway there, he doubted whether leaving the building had been such a good idea. Wouldn't Sally come to him, assuming she still could? Given that he had all the time in the world, wasn't this impatience? Despite all the intervening aggravation, he didn't think it was long ago that he marched out to this exact spot, to move the bin. Half a dozen hours of aggravation would be nothing, compared to her experience.

The woman's face was cast slightly downward. Her head was covered in a black headscarf and, below that, she wore a dark sweater. A single, thin ring was visible on her left hand. Her dark blue jeans were becoming damp at the hem, along with her trainers.

The air was cool on Jason's face. Too much thinking found him almost colliding with her.

"Excuse me, do you have the time?" he said quickly.

She checked her watch, without looking up. A large number

was swept aside for two pairs of digits, separated by a colon.

"A quarter past ten," responded the woman, who carried on, without even looking at him.

He returned to the building and sat on the edge of the threshold, wondering what to do. Should he head out or wait? He watched the door close behind him. Only in a dream could the building have faded away with none of this having ever happened. Then, like Sally had done, he kept looking at the building over his shoulder as he walked away. It had such an impact in his life. He had no one to wave to but he still turned. It was a warm, sunny day and there were a few people here and there.

He crossed the tarmac of the car park and noted his house, away to his left. He thought of turning and walking past it. Beyond the house and the rest of those familiar roads, was another estate. It had been constructed on the far side of the main road and adjacent to the petrol station. It contained the same type of houses, from what he could see of it. Less moss on the roofs was about the only difference. Same houses, same people. All strangers in this place. Like him. There was no back-up plan. Not to mention, he was looking for a person he hadn't met. A woman. She might not even be around. Should he return to the time when the last stripe was painted?

As he walked on, he saw a few people in the park. Some were walking along the path, ahead. There was someone on the swings, behind that colourful metal fence with the items to entertain but unbalance children. The football strips of the children playing were broadly similar to the ones he remembered. More parents watched over their children than there used to be, when he'd played.

As he walked towards the road, without any direction in mind, he focused on the person on the swings. It was only when he was alongside her, that he realised it was a woman. She wore a largely white, short dress, patterned with many red roses, on top of a pair of dark green jeans. She wore sandals, no socks. She wasn't really swinging. It was more of a rocking. He wondered if he should talk to her, though he was wary she might ask him about something current.

"Lovely day," he offered.

"Just like any other," came a reply.

"Do you live here?" he enquired.

"Not anymore. You?"

"I used to. Years ago."

He was aware of the meaning of that. He looked in the direction of the building. It was all messed up. What had happened to his father, Mrs G and his friends at school? And what of Simon? He caught his lips between a thumb and forefinger, then squeezed them to prevent any words from coming out. As he turned, he was taken aback to find the woman standing there, right in front of him.

"Hello Jason. Those clothes must be twelve years out of date by now," said Sally.

She grabbed him fiercely and held him, for a long time. When they parted, he could see now the similarities and the differences. He hadn't been looking. Not properly.

"You're early. We were supposed to meet at noon. I was readying myself."

"Let's sit down."

She took his hand and led him back to the swings. There they both rocked back and forth. There was no conversation, for a while. Questions abounded in his head and he was sure there were just as many answers in hers. What had happened in the last twelve years? Did Abigail come along? Had Sally met anyone else? So many questions, but where to start?

He had to keep looking at her. Her transformation had been

as sudden as his must have been to her. As he looked at her, there were no feelings. He wasn't even frustrated by their absence. And what about hers? Did she still care for him, as she said she would? She'd been prepared to take that chance. Considering the change in him, she'd gone out on a limb, in assuming it would all work out. She'd grown into a woman and was still beautiful. There was a 'but', which he didn't want to admit to.

She began to speak and then stopped. She looked down and around, perhaps searching for the words. They came, falteringly at first, as if she was saying them out loud for the first time. At times, there was fluency. At others, it was a one-sided brainstorm with ideas floating out.

"It's been a long time, waiting for you to come home. I bet you remember everything like it was yesterday. Today, even. You were right about the interviews. So many questions. So many faces asking the same things. I doubted myself. I knew I was doing it for us, though, so my focus remained true. My parents were no help, but we knew that, anyway."

She turned her face away. "Simon didn't last much longer. I went to see him, before the end. I told him we'd gone looking, to find out what had happened to him. I think he reacted when I held his hand but I don't know if he heard me. His mother moved to a different part of town, about a year later. I helped her pack. I see her around, sometimes, but we don't talk. I think she's trying to move on. Your dad hung on for another two years, until work took him away. We talked a lot and he helped me through lots of things at school and with my parents. He's a good listener and I miss him. I knew he was thinking about moving. Then, one day, I came home from school and found he'd just gone. Left, with no way of contacting him. Caitlin moved away the day after she hit sixteen. She'd been planning it for a while. There was no Abi."

She stopped talking and the silence returned. The background of frivolity elsewhere in the park didn't interrupt their scene. When Jason started to speak, she held up a hand and carried on.

"It's been a long time. It took me a long time to realise it was all my fault."

He tried to interrupt but she was there, first. Her voice was weary. It was tiring for her to run through this, one last time.

"If you stop me now, I might never say this out loud, so please, give me the time. I couldn't help myself. On the day Simon disappeared, I was in love with you. That shiny hair. Your adventurous spirit. But he had angered you. It made me think you felt it, too and strongly. In the embarrassment of being revealed, you tried to lock the stable door."

"That's where it all started."

"No, it was me, and most nights I think about Simon and you. Yes, you were coming back, but not for a long time. So many nights I wanted to come to the building to try and find you. So many days I sat where we used to sit, looking at the window, wondering how to climb in, alone. Sometimes, I took Caitlin. I thought she could help me but I always lost my nerve. After all, it was a secret and, if she found out, other people might, too. I think she saw her older sister becoming more obsessed. I told my parents we were out at study group. Instead, I was out there, wishing for you to leave. I painted the white line on the tree in the hope you'd step out. You didn't. I cried for us. I cried for the future that is to come and the fall of Earth. All down to me telling them everything. I can't reconcile myself to it. We agreed to meet here, today, and here I am.

"When you walked up here, I said I don't live here, anymore because I am off to work for a charity, overseas. Perhaps, somewhere down the road, I can atone for this. I have longed for the day when I can be with someone who had been through the same things as me. I've turned away the chance of love because I was afraid of letting someone down. I was afraid of what I had already lost."

She stood up from the swing and looked at him.

"You don't know how much you have missed. It is one thing to grow up abroad and not be a part of the community but at least you're aware of it. But you're different. You're waking up from a coma and there's only a few links between now and when you left. So many events, so many references will be meaningless. You are a stranger in your own home."

Standing up, Jason responded, "I hear you."

"I don't think you do. You're dead. Or you died. You don't exist. You lived just over there but you're not a native. You're not even a stranger in town. Neither are you an immigrant or a refugee. You are nothing. You have no identity. You're out of your time. Imagine trying to start a new life in Mikey's time. We didn't have a crystal. There will be questions.

"They are here now. We opened the door and they used it. They misused it to send back their waste, to build their armada without the watchful eyes of the Alliance.

He watched her for a few moments, as she endeavoured to deliver a speech she had been working on for a while.

She touched the back of her head as she continued.

"We both received biological implants. That's how we picked up the training so fast."

Jason wondered how she knew all this. They'd been separated only once, that he remembered and that had been during his first flight. He saw a chance to reduce some of the pain.

"It wasn't just me or you. It was both of us. You said you divulged information. Don't forget you told me and that memory is more recent, for me. You don't recall doing it and it could have been done without our knowledge. I got us into the building and I was determined to go down that first flight of stairs. We had no idea what was involved. Yes, a lot of people died but they didn't die at our hands."

There was more. There was always more to say.

"It was both of us," he finished. "It was me. I rushed off. Well, not exactly. If I'd stayed, I wouldn't have been touched by that green field. We could have come home together."

He looked into her eyes. She nodded to accept his words but her heart had already convinced her. She carried on talking to him. She explained it was years before someone dared to look through all the walls she'd put up. To see past the stigma of losing the only two friends that had meant a damn to her. She told Jason she'd turned him away, but he didn't give up.

"He was everything I needed. He was tall, handsome – nice breath, even – with a lovely smile and he stayed. But a small part of me was still waiting for you. He moved on and I regret that, daily. If you had died, as Simon did, I would have moved on but I didn't. I couldn't. I know you knew that when I left. I could see it in your eyes but you couldn't tell me. I think I understand now.

"I loved you from the beginning and I think you loved me, but you weren't ready to show it. You had to rush off after Simon, then you had to rush off to fight some species you'd never heard of. You could have been killed, lost an arm, hit a mine and left barely a speck of dust in the cosmos to recognise you by. Did you even see an alien? You wanted to save the world. Congratulations, you're a hero, except your audience won't be born for millennia."

"They were an advanced civilisation."

"Advanced? Technologically, maybe. But humanity is no better off. Is kidnapping children to fight your war the ideals of an advanced culture? Think about us. Our civilisation has cars, planes and satellites. To the Bronze Age people we lived with, those are things beyond their imagination. They're tools that we use. It doesn't make us advanced."

Jason admitted, "I didn't want to go. They tricked me."

Jason knew it all hinged on her. It all depended on returning to her. The girl he had loved. Neither of them moved but he could see them further apart than when he'd walked up here. She was right. He had all of history and all of the future at his disposal, but there was nowhere or no-when into which he fit. There was no Jason-sized hole in this time.

She invited him to her house. Her parents were away with relatives, for a few days. Sally had told them she'd arranged for her girlfriends to come over, for the evening. She had even invited a couple but then cancelled, last night. It was going to be a post-university celebration. Jason found walking down that road was awkward. Mrs G's door wasn't that bright red, anymore. It was a more a faded green that could have been a door at the hospital. His house had other people pottering around, in the garden. What did they know about living in his house?

They sat on the settee and talked.

"I think my sister could see I was being driven mad by the whole thing. She told me it was all in the past and I should let it go. It's not normal to hold on to it. She was right."

Sally told her parents she was going away for a year. She told them it was the new thing, to do it after university instead of before. She hadn't told them she wasn't coming home. She hadn't told anyone. She asked him to promise not to tell. He said he wouldn't tell a soul. Who could he tell?

In the end, they were barely friends. This was a social arrangement. He was surprised when she kissed him and led him upstairs. It was the 'but' he had encountered as soon as he saw her. Yes, she was beautiful, but she was so different from how he'd remembered her. She wasn't the girl with whom he had fallen in love. He wondered if he could fall in love again. She was going away and not coming back. She wasn't even the same person. She had changed so much and quickly, to his eyes, as he had done to her. They were two broken souls and neither knew how to repair the damage. There was no further contact during the night or at breakfast in the morning.

Had she rejected him, first? Had she placed it all on this one night and then to escape to wherever? If they'd had a week, maybe there would have been the time for both of them. She'd already decided to leave, so why should he become involved? The planned departure for a life of giving to others, to atone for sins no one could ever comprehend. Perhaps, she was taking back control. Making that decision for herself. A new place. A new mind. Would he ever see her again? Something told him he would not. Once, they were ready to die with each other. And they nearly did. How was he so ready to throw his life away but not speak his mind?

After breakfast, she had a little spare money and offered him enough to feed himself for a day. She insisted and pressed it into his hands. She hugged him one last time, as the bus approached. It would take her to the train station and beyond. The penultimate glance and she handed him something. Jason looked down and found a data storage device in his palm.

"I've written about the building. I thought it would help. No one else could understand. No one but you and you weren't around. Talking about it, writing about it, revealed things to me. Things buried, things I hadn't been aware of. You should write your side, too. Don't leave it too late. Don't look for your father, or anyone else you used to know. As far as they're concerned, you are dead. What would you do if your mother suddenly turned up? It's all secured on there. The pin number is your birthday."

He nodded slowly.

"Stay with me," he asked. "At least until I'm set up."

"My plane leaves this evening. A ticket is being held for me. I need to do this. I need to be away."

They waited by the roadside in silence and she offered one last look into his eyes.

"Do you remember that time, on the stairs? When we'd escaped the fire. You were upset about your mum. You said it took a while before you missed her. I'd be willing to bet you missed her more then, not because you loved her more but because you understood love more. I look into your eyes now and see that boy is long gone. But that's only a part of it. The love inside you has gone. You have a determination in your eyes but not a sparkle. Maybe it's a blessing. You'll feel no pain."

As the bus pulled up, there was a pressurised release of air as the door was opened. They looked at each other one last time. As soon as she stepped on, he might as well not have existed, which she had assured him was true. He tried to wave as the bus pulled away but her eyes were on the future.

He realised, later, he should have fought for it. He could have tried harder but he didn't. Right up to the moment where she stepped on the bus, he could have asked her to stay – and not just for a week – but he didn't. Was that why she zoned out, on the bus? She probably knew it was over and she had made the right choice to leave. They could have found a place. Made a go of it. Options came and went. He wanted to catch the next bus, go after her, but time had passed by then. Maybe she had waited for him at the station and hoped he would catch up with her. He imagined her waiting for him, then asking what had taken him so long. If he was wrong, he would be chasing after rainbows, dreams and wishes. In the moment, it all seemed too much. He didn't even know where she was going. He hadn't asked. Another *what if*. In truth, he knew he could never be sure, if she would have stayed. As the day wore on, he wondered how he might go about finding her again. Aside from knocking on the door of her parents' house, which he would never do.

They may have looked the same age but they were a time apart. Sally had grown up without him and endured much. She'd seen his dad's and Mrs G's grief drive them from their homes. She passed up at least one good chance of romance, saving herself for a memory. They both had scars. Twelve years ago, they'd been similar but no more. Wounds hadn't healed. They embraced and, for their own reasons, released pain in their own way. Sally had walked away. He had let her go. This was the same person whom he had seen run away from him, only hours ago. The one who promised to wait for him and had done. What had he done about it? You can only hold onto that dream for so long. She'd asked him if he knew how many times she'd come back to him, in those long, lonely years.

"I needed you but you weren't there," she'd said.

The money she'd given him didn't last long. He told himself there must be a way out but every turn revealed another hurdle. You can't have an identity without an address and you can't move into an address without an identity – a card, preferably one with a photograph and a signature.

"Does sir not have a passport or a driving licence to apply for this benefit?"

Long queues twisted round the floor to reach that point. Tutting and harrumphing sounds from behind when he had dawdled.

"You can apply through our website," he was advised, then herded out of the way.

In response to his lack of access, he was told to try the library, except for that he needed money to use the computers, which he didn't have. He tried begging, but he looked too well and received only verbal feedback. The suit was helping him survive.

He had grown up, partially, just up the road. But who was

he? He had the name that his dad had given him but no place to live, no income and no food beyond what was in his pockets. He trudged around for a couple of days, periodically sucking on an energy bar. He tried to figure out what to do. He wondered where Sally was. A plane ticket, she'd said. There was no way of finding her. He couldn't go back in time. There'd be two of him in one space and that wouldn't work.

This led his thoughts back to the building. He wondered if it could offer him some shelter and buy him a little time. Perhaps he could live in the lower levels and eat from the box, until he had an idea or a plan. Maybe he could dip in and out, when he needed to. He didn't want to go back there. He had walked through the park with uncertainty on his mind.

There was no one in sight. He opted for a bold approach, rather than sneaking. Simon used to say unusual movement can draw the eye to you. He wondered about changing the suit's appearance to blend with the background but the coast looked clear. The windows were reflective but he could still see through them enough to know there was no one in. The smell in the air and its taste in his throat slowed him to a stop, then he backed off a step. He knew what he was going to do and how to climb in. He'd done it often enough. He was a little larger than the first time he tried it but that shouldn't slow things up, noticeably.

Deep breath and forward. As he placed his hands on the window to push it up, he received an electric shock that staggered him. He withdrew his hands instantly but the discharge had gone through his chest, and he stumbled backwards to the ground. He sat there, waiting for the sensations to subside. The window opened slowly and he moved back on all fours while keeping it in view. Once it stopped moving, there was a blurring and a middle-aged man appeared in the room. As he looked at the face, most of it was of an older man but the lips and the ears looked out of place. There was a grey thread of hair on his head.

"Hello, young Jason," he said. "Well, youngish. Good to see you again."

Jason had seen that face only a few days ago and hadn't expected to see it, ever again. The base of the window opened upwards and Jason could only see in if he remained sitting down. On the one hand, he was fine with this, for now because he was still recovering from the shock. On the other, it gave the man the psychological advantage of being higher.

"Surprised to see me?"

Jason nodded.

"I don't know why. You and I both know what this place is capable of."

The man leaned forward to have a better look at him sitting on the floor. As he did so, his hands came to rest on the frame. Jason made no great show of noticing. He pushed his hands off the ground and rolled forward onto his haunches. Within a second, he launched himself towards the gap. The man didn't even move, but Jason did. He was flung a yard further back than where he'd sat a moment before.

"What was that?" Jason demanded.

"Personal defence field, hand-held weapon, random chance of touching the building as the charge came by? You decide. You might even pick the right answer."

Behind the man, two people were working behind screens. Knight dismissed them from the room then informed Jason about their task.

"To ensure you both entered and left the building. After that, they've been checking the gases from our construction below is leaving in the right amounts."

When Jason said he hadn't noticed anyone around when he'd left, he was quick to step in.

"Which means they did a fine job. One of their duties was to pop a newspaper into the bin, to ensure you left at the right time. Good show to them, don't you agree? While camouflaged, of course, they could come up and down as they pleased, without your awareness."

The man seemed to want to talk. Maybe there was a weakness within the defences, somewhere. Jason dropped the fire-first attitude and moved to questions.

"Why did you do this?"

"It's our building, now. The future is set."

"A future that ends in the destruction of Earth?"

"All part of the plan. They are determined to destroy the Earth, so we plan to let them. The solar system, after the planet's destruction, will be a gravitational anomaly. Zero jumps will tear up the local space. You wouldn't think it was possible to take a whole piece of nothing, put something in it, only to remove it utterly but leave something behind. Accidents showed us what was possible."

Jason thought back to Ki-Tae and the ship that never came home. Was it an accident?

"Of the enemy ships that will assail the Earth, some will escape, some will be destroyed and most will be damaged. Those that survive the encounter at Earth in mostly one piece, will be trapped. We created a cage of gravitational seams, from which escape will be dangerous in normal travel and deadly in jump space. We don't have to kill them all, we only needed to lock them in."

"Why are you telling me this?"

"Aren't you proud? Earth won. Humanity will live on. In fact, humans will live on another planet."

Jason noticed he seemed pleased with himself.

"We lifted the entire species from one place to another. If you and your friends had not discovered the power of this place, we would not have seized the initiative."

"By seizing the initiative, you mean starting a war and killing millions of people?

"More than that, I suspect but, yes, fights start. People are hurt. If only there were the means to have our way, without the death. There isn't. We minimise what we can, on our side. What about your world wars? How many dead, wounded and moved on, by both sides?"

"They're not my wars." Jason thought he was being attacked.

"They're of your time. You remember them, annually. We are already in the process of moving to a properly new and clean planet on which we can survive, once a number of issues are resolved."

"What's going on in your time?"

"Ha! My boy, that almost has no meaning for me, anymore."

Boy. Whose boy was he now?

"You were a projection when I last saw you a few days ago. Transmitted from *New Earth*. About to become digital, like the lady."

"Ah, we had only considered putting that process in place, for her. It's good to know it worked. Thank you for the advanced knowledge. I'll see you stay out of trouble, for that."

Jason had a couple more thoughts.

"Is it too late to join the fight for Earth?"

"Much too late, sir. Benefit of the somewhat niche hindsight we have, in this organisation. You will try to bring down *The Project*."

"You choose not to let me in now?"

"Now or later. No chance. We've seen the damage you've done in here, so I'm here to ensure it never happens. Suffice to say you were creative, after you found an abettor. But that's all been undone. Now would be a good time to look to your right and then your left."

Jason did so and found two policemen rounding the corners. Jason's shoulders slumped.

"This is public ground, you can't do this," he said with certainty.

"The footpath is on the other side. This side is trespassing. I wouldn't recommend running. They *will* catch you, after the one on your left stuns you."

"Run or not run. What can I do with myself? I'm just another one of your victims."

"A fine recourse, for all the training we gave you."

"Piloting skills in space? Hardly useful, right now."

"Before you flew and as you grew into the man, the link expanded your knowledge on lots of things. All those subjects you hate and so much more, besides. All uploaded quickly. You have another chance. Try not to throw this one away."

Jason unconsciously raised a hand to the nape of his skull as he listened. He felt nothing. The man's eyes refocused on him.

"All those school years without the pain of going to school and more, besides. In this new path, you will find me partially grateful for your services. Not enough to give you what you want – that is, to let you in. Rather, I will offer you what you need, which these two fine gentlemen will provide. The Queen will continue to rule and more will join her in that centre." He regarded Jason, as the two uniformed men each placed a hand on his arms. "For you, this game is at an end."

To the policemen he said, "This man is somewhat confused. I do not wish to press charges, on this occasion. However, I would greatly appreciate it if you could find out who he is and where he is from. I think he needs a place to stay and a warm meal. Thank you."

Jason was led away. They walked around the corner, where he saw their car, alone in the parking area. As they transferred to the tarmac, one of the men released his grip while the other tightened his. One of them offered Jason a drink. He replied with a subdued affirmation and was given a cup of tea from a flask. Jason subconsciously called this one 'Mikey'. He recalled an old conversation, as the tea pourer sat down on the passenger seat and activated their computer.

He could do with Sally, right now, to help him figure this out. He wasn't rushing anywhere but it was her brains he missed. Simon's too. It wouldn't work without them but it was unlikely they were coming back. I need you. Both of you. Where are you?

"Let's start with the basics. What's your name?" said PC Mikey.

A cloud moved past. Sunlight from the summer sun reflected from the window on the rear door of the car and flashed onto Jason's face. It momentarily blinded him and he recoiled. As he opened his eyes from the flare, he cast a rueful look back to the building. He closed them for a moment longer and felt the touch of the flickering sun on his eyelids.

CHAPTER 18

How could he? How could he!

The red mist had gone up and Jason set off after Simon, who responded quickly to the flash in his friend's eyes. Fire burned deep from Jason's heart to his skin and triggered all the adrenal glands along the route. His legs drove up and down, like pistons and powered his body forward in extremely hot pursuit. He sensed the gap widening and the engine room called for more coals. His predator eyes saw only Simon, who changed course. Now he was aiming for the rear of the building, encased in its shield of scaffolding. Sally's image filtered into his mind and he stopped. Jason knew he'd never catch him. Simon's feet were faster than his. Here he stood in a no-man's land between the friend who'd betrayed him and the girl he couldn't stop thinking about. He didn't know whether to go forward or back and he simply stood. A piece of a puzzle trying to figure out where to fit itself in.

I'll make a fool of myself.

That stupid building. None of the adults liked it and never went near. Today had been just another day, until Simon dropped that bombshell almost casually, as if it was old news. He hadn't realised he was talking out loud, until her voice from behind responded.

"Jason." "Was it true, what Simon said?"

Jason hesitated. There was nowhere to hide. He nodded. Sally's voice continued.

"Simon said it. It would be nice if you could."

The heat of the anger pulled away to reveal the heat of the embarrassment waiting underneath. Words battled against each other for the response to save face or accept the truth. It had just happened, one day. That day when he hadn't responded to Simon quickly enough and he knew. How did he know? Now, he found himself vulnerable and expecting the worst.

It's what you want. Just say it. Tell her.

"I love you, Sally."

He felt her hand touch his, then he heard her soft voice again.

"It's a start. I look forward to the time when you look at me, as you say it."

His face still bright red, he turned to her and smiled. She looked good. No, better than good. He hadn't really noticed just how much, until recently. He hadn't told a soul but that sort of thing didn't stop Simon. He would be a detective when he was older. Jason knew what he should say but didn't know how to say it. He had been waiting for the right time. Simon advanced the programme. In the absence of further comment, Sally derailed his internal dialogue.

"Aren't you chasing him?"

"I don't chase boys," he muttered, barely audibly, just over his breath.

"You seemed so keen, just a moment ago."

He was about to respond but chose instead to breathe in and out, slowly. Up ahead, his friend looked back through the scaffolding. He turned to look at her and, for a moment, no words were uttered.

She overtook him, stopped and turned to face him. Her eyes radiated a sunshine that would be with him for all of time. He didn't know how long that was but now was enough for him.

Light flashed into his eyes as Simon opened the window at the back of the building. The afternoon sun snuck out from behind a cloud and Jason shied his head away from the glare. When he turned back, it was with a raised hand to block the source of the light. Simon seemed to have taken a grip of the frame and his shoes fought for purchase on the wall.

"You're very pretty," he said at last.

Just as the engine cooled down a notch, his idiot brain threw another shovel-load of coal into the fire. It was a short sentence and felt hard to say but it needed saying.

"Thank you," she replied before adding, "You don't mind then?"

"Mind what?"

"Only, Simon made a similar observation, before you charged after him."

"I didn't like the way he put it."

"That was obvious!" She laughed, then patted his wrist. Smiling, she followed it up with, "I preferred your way."

♙♟♟♟♟♙

Simon stood there, his thick, black curly hair buffeted by the gentle breeze. He smiled as he watched the happy couple learning to hold hands. It was probably a bit early to expect them to do much more. Poor little Jason. Does he know what he's let himself in for? He'd have to be a little more careful, in the future. Jason blew hot and cold but Simon hadn't expected that explosion. Simon surprised himself that he'd decided to run. It was probably the fire from one of the lower levels of hell in his friend's eyes that did it. Jason's heart was in the right place though.

Aside from that, Simon was pleased with today's turn of events. Next on the list was to enlighten Jason about Sally's father, the rising star in the council. His mum told him there was a man who needed to be brought down a peg or two. He had an idea but he could do with Jason's help. Within a couple of minutes, the pair caught up with him. He was standing around with his hands on his hips as if he'd been waiting all day. He didn't speak but looked a bit fidgety. A moment ago, his best friend had all but declared war on him but now, as they approached, he offered only a smile.

Yes, save the energy. You'll need it. Simon smiled back.

They were veering away and heading towards the stile. He called Jason over with the promise of an open window to investigate. There was a bit of hesitation, which was promising, before they parted. Sally remained at the corner as Jason jogged up.

"She's staying on guard in case anyone comes along."

Simon sensed an opportunity.

"Who? Your girlfriend?"

Jason looked up at him with a frown, then swapped it for a smile. Simon's nose picked up an oddity in the air and grunted.

"Do you recognise that smell?"

"Probably the glue they use to stick cheap carpet to the floor. My dad took me to his work one weekend. They had the same smell."

"Your dad lives at work. Is he trying to hide from someone?" Simon retorted, then regretted it. That Jason hadn't noticed made him feel worse.

"It's definitely brown in there," his friend observed. "It's a bit of a throwback to a bygone age. Not the Bronze Age but the Boring Age."

"Hah! That's about right. There are other things we could do."

There was a tingle in his fingers. The sensation of risk, of being somewhere without permission, of discovering something. In spite of Jason's summary of the beige world within, there could be something worth their attention. He looked at Jason, who was more interested in what was at the end of the building. He had taken a step back and Simon wondered if he could even climb in. Simon sensed the hesitation in his friend and offered a challenge.

"If you don't fancy it, I can check it on my own."

For a moment he looked caught between two thoughts and soon settled on one.

"The sun's out. I don't fancy being indoors." A few seconds later, he added, "Adults have been in there, how exciting is it going to be? I mean, it was built on a field. It probably smells of cows in there."

It was Simon's turn to look sharply at his friend. He stared for a moment at Jason, who had turned to look at her. He smiled.

My little friend has grown up a little. No time left for secrets in buildings. There are enough secrets in us now.

Simon felt it was beneath him but he did want to test his friend one last time to be sure.

"I suppose you've no time for this sort of thing now?"

The look that came back could have knocked him down with a feather. Jason wasn't interested.

"Have fun in there. We'll wait outside."

Good answer.

Simon decided to close it. He pushed the window but it was stuck on something high up, which he reported back to Jason.

"Aren't you tall enough to reach it?"

"Give me a leg up and I'll see what I can do about it."

"Not until you show me the bottom of your shoes."

Simon laughed. "That only happened once."

"Once too often."

The scaffolding wasn't close enough to the building to do what he wanted. The extra height advantage, from the one with the least to offer, gave him the reach he needed to pull it all free.

Once it was all clear to his satisfaction, he pushed it, pulled it, poked at the catches and pushed it shut hard. It clicked shut.

In the warmth of the afternoon sun, Jason shivered.

"Someone walked over your grave?" enquired Simon.

Jason nodded. "It felt really odd there."

"Me too. I think that's a good sign that we didn't go in."

Simon looked around to see if anyone had seen them. Even closing the window could still look a bit shifty. Someone approaching at the wrong time might assume they had just climbed out. When he looked back, Jason was already halfway to Sally.

"What was all that about? Why did you close the window?" she said to Simon, as the three of them were reunited.

"If we're not going in there, no one is."

The light flickered across Jason's eyes and he looked up towards the sky to see wisps of clouds skitter in front of the sun.

"Sally?" he said unexpectedly.

"Yes, Jason. Are you all right?"

"I was just distracted for a moment." He looked up at the tor, which used to be a fort in the days before the Romans came.

Sally followed his eyes and offered, "Shall we go for a walk up there?"

"Do you have time?" Jason asked her.

"Probably not but let's go anyway."

As the three of them joined, Simon moved ahead a few paces. He looked back and saw Jason wasn't interested. He waited for them to draw alongside, then tagged along. With the sun behind them, they followed their shadows towards their destinations.

ABOUT THE AUTHOR

Clive Stephens was born in India in the 1970s. His interest in science fiction came from reading Pratchett, Eddings and Asimov. He has a science background that stems from two engineering diplomas.

He joined a writing group in 2018 and had a short story published the following year. *The Restoration Project: Forfeit* follows on from his first novel, *Gambit*, and second novel *Variant*. Forfeit is the third and final instalment in the trilogy. He has spent most of his life in Buckinghamshire and lives there today.

www.ingramcontent.com/pod-product-compliance
Lightning Source LLC
Chambersburg PA
CBHW060354080526
44583CB00012B/307